Communications
in Computer and Information Science 453

More information about this series at http://www.springer.com/series/7899

Markus Helfert · Frédéric Desprez
Donald Ferguson · Frank Leymann (Eds.)

Cloud Computing and Services Science

Third International Conference, CLOSER 2013
Aachen, Germany, May 8–10, 2013
Revised Selected Papers

 Springer

Editors
Markus Helfert
Dublin City University
Dublin
Ireland

Frédéric Desprez
LIP/Inria
Le Chesnay
France

Donald Ferguson
Dell
Round Rock
USA

Frank Leymann
University of Stuttgart
Stuttgart
Germany

ISSN 1865-0929   ISSN 1865-0937 (electronic)
ISBN 978-3-319-11560-3   ISBN 978-3-319-11561-0 (eBook)
DOI 10.1007/978-3-319-11561-0

Library of Congress Control Number: 2014949555

Springer Cham Heidelberg New York Dordrecht London

Printed on acid-free paper

Springer is part of Springer Science+Business Media (www.springer.com)

Preface

This book includes extended and revised versions of a set of selected papers from CLOSER 2013 (the 3rd International Conference on Cloud Computing and Services Science), held in Aachen, Germany, in 2013, and organized by the Institute for Systems and Technologies of Information, Control and Communication (INSTICC) and co-organized by RWTH Aachen University. The conference was also technically sponsored by SINTEF, International Federation for Information Processing (IFIP) and IEEE Cloud Computing.

The purpose of the CLOSER series of conferences is to bring together researchers, engineers, and practitioners interested in the emerging area of cloud computing. The conference has four main tracks, namely "Cloud Computing Fundamentals", "Services Science Foundation for Cloud Computing", "Cloud Computing Platforms and applications", and "Cloud Computing Enabling Technology".

CLOSER 2013 received 142 paper submissions from all continents. From these, 26 papers were presented as full papers, 24 were accepted as short papers and another 29 for poster presentation at the conference. These numbers, leading to a full-paper acceptance ratio of 18% and an oral paper acceptance ratio of 35%, show the intention of preserving a high quality forum for the next editions of this conference. Out of these, 8 papers were selected for presentation in this volume.

This book contains the revised papers selected among the best contributions taking also into account the quality of their presentation at the conference, assessed by session chairs. Therefore, we hope that you find these papers interesting, and we trust they may represent a helpful reference for all those who need to address any of the research areas above mentioned.

We wish to thank all those who supported and helped to organize the conference. On behalf of the conference Organizing Committee, we would like to thank the authors, whose work mostly contributed to a very successful conference and to the members of the Program Committee, whose expertise and diligence were instrumental to ensure the quality of final contributions. We also wish to thank all the members of the Organizing Committee whose work and commitment was invaluable. Last but not least, we would like to thank Springer for their collaboration in getting this book to print.

December 2013

Markus Helfert
Frédéric Desprez
Donald Ferguson
Frank Leymann

Organization

Conference Co-chairs

Matthias Jarke	RWTH Aachen, Germany
Markus Helfert	Dublin City University, Ireland

Program Co-chairs

Frédéric Desprez	LIP/Inria, France
Donald Ferguson	Dell, USA
Ethan Hadar	AGT International, Switzerland
Frank Leymann	University of Stuttgart, Germany

Organizing Committee

Marina Carvalho	INSTICC, Portugal
Helder Coelhas	INSTICC, Portugal
Bruno Encarnação	INSTICC, Portugal
Ana Guerreiro	INSTICC, Portugal
André Lista	INSTICC, Portugal
Andreia Moita	INSTICC, Portugal
Carla Mota	INSTICC, Portugal
Raquel Pedrosa	INSTICC, Portugal
Vitor Pedrosa	INSTICC, Portugal
Ana Ramalho	INSTICC, Portugal
Susana Ribeiro	INSTICC, Portugal
Sara Santiago	INSTICC, Portugal
Mara Silva	INSTICC, Portugal
José Varela	INSTICC, Portugal
Pedro Varela	INSTICC, Portugal

Program Committee

Ron Addie, Australia
Antonia Albani, Switzerland
Vasilios Andrikopoulos, Germany
Joseph Antony, Australia
Claudio Ardagna, Italy
Danilo Ardagna, Italy
Liliana Ardissono, Italy
Alvaro Arenas, Spain
Benjamin Aziz, UK
Zeina Azmeh, France
Amelia Badica, Romania
Janaka Balasooriya, USA

Luis M. Vaquero, UK
Massimo Villari, Italy
Mladen A. Vouk, USA
Hiroshi Wada, Australia
Maria Emilia M. T.Walter, Brazil
Lizhe Wang, China
Martijn Warnier, The Netherlands

Sven Wenzel, Germany
Jan-Jan Wu, Taiwan
Hany F. El Yamany, Egypt
Bo Yang, China
Ustun Yildiz, USA
Zhifeng Yun, USA
Michael Zapf, Germany

Auxiliary Reviewers

David Allison, Canada
Suhair Alshehri, USA
Nick van Beest, The Netherlands
Dario Bruneo, Italy
Werner Buck, The Netherlands
Roberto Cascella, France
Antonio Celesti, Italy
Philip Church, Australia
Kassidy Clark, The Netherlands
Alexandru Costan, France
Mozhdeh Gholobeigi, Italy
Antonios Gouglidis, Greece
Katarina Grolinger, Canada
Wubin Li, Sweden
Francesco Longo, Italy

Diego Magro, Italy
Gael Le Mahec, France
Mario Marino, Italy
Dimitrios Michalopoulos, Greece
Giuseppe Di Modica, Italy
Faris Nizamic, The Netherlands
M. Mustafa Rafique, Ireland
Eduardo Roloff, Brazil
Cyril Seguin, France
Manuel Stein, Germany
Pawel Szmeja, Poland
Atsuko Takefusa, Japan
Genoveva Vargas-Solar, France
Zhi Wang, USA
Katarzyna Wasielewska, Poland

Invited Speakers

Gottfried Vossen
Ivona Brandic
Geoffrey Charles Fox

WWU Münster, Germany
Vienna UT, Austria
Indiana University, USA

Contents

SecLA-Based Negotiation and Brokering of Cloud Resources

Jesus Luna[1], Tsvetoslava Vateva-Gurova[2(✉)], Neeraj Suri[2],
Massimiliano Rak[3], and Alessandra De Benedictis[4]

[1] Cloud Security Alliance, Scotland, UK
jluna@cloudsecurityalliance.org
[2] Department of Computer Science, Technische Universität Darmstadt,
Darmstadt, Germany
{vateva,suri}@deeds.informatik.tu-darmstadt.de
[3] Dipartimento di Ingegneria Dell'Informazione, Seconda Universita' di Napoli,
Caserta, Italy
massimiliano.rak@unina2.it
[4] Department of Electrical Engineering and Information Technology,
University of Naples Federico II, Napoli, Italy
alessandra.debenedictis@unina.it

Abstract. As the popularity of Cloud computing has grown during the last years, the choice of Cloud Service Provider (CSP) has become an important issue from user's perspective. Although the Cloud users are more and more concerned about their security in the Cloud and might have some specific security requirements, currently this choice is based on requirements related to the offered Service Level Agreements (SLA) and costs. Most of the CSPs do not provide user- understandable information regarding the security levels associated with their services, and in this way impede the users to negotiate their security requirements. In other words, the users do not have the technical means in terms of tools and semantics to choose the CSP that best suits their security demands. Industrial efforts on specification of Cloud security parameters in SLAs, also known as "Security Level Agreements" or SecLAs represent the initial steps towards solving this problem. The aim of this paper is to propose a practical approach that enables user-centric negotiation and brokering of Cloud resources. The proposed methodology relies on both the notion of SecLAs for establishing a common semantic between the CSPs and the users, and on a quantitative approach to evaluate the security levels associated with the specific SecLAs.

This work is a result of the joint effort spent on the security metrology-related techniques being developed by the EU FP7 projects ABC4Trust/ SPECS and, the framework for SLA-based negotiation and Cloud resource brokering proposed by the EU FP7 mOSAIC project. The feasibility of the proposed negotiation approach and its applicability for Cloud Federations is demonstrated in the paper with a real-world case study considering a scenario presented in the FP7 project SPECS. The presented scenario shows the negotiation of a user's security requirements with respect to a set of CSPs SecLAs, using both the information

© Springer International Publishing Switzerland 2014
M. Helfert et al. (Eds.): CLOSER 2013, CCIS 453, pp. 1–18, 2014.
DOI: 10.1007/978-3-319-11561-0_1

available in the Cloud Security Alliance's "Security, Trust & Assurance Registry" (CSA STAR) and the WS-Agreement standard.

Keywords: Cloud security · Security level agreements · Security metrics · Security negotiation · Resource brokering

1   Introduction

While the many economic and technological advantages of Cloud computing are apparent, the migration of key security relevant applications onto it has been limited, in part, due to the lack of accountable *security assurance* specification provided by the Cloud Service Provider. Furthermore, the typical Cloud user is not a security expert, though nevertheless has specific security requirements to fulfill (e.g., due to regulatory compliance) that are usually expressed at an informal level, thus making them difficult and expensive to align and negotiate with respect to the CSP's security offer. Unfortunately, at the state of practice (e.g., as discussed by the Cloud Security Alliance's SLA WG [1]), many Cloud users find themselves without the means to match and further negotiate their security requirements with available CSPs. Contrary to Cloud resource negotiation based on non-security indicators (e.g., using performance metrics as presented in [2]), the field of security-based negotiation presents several challenges mainly due to both the lack of security assurance/quantifiers, and the *semantic gap* among users and CSPs with respect to security.

Fortunately, security negotiation in Cloud computing has recently taken some initial and promising steps. Early academic works like [3] and, the Cloud community (e.g., workgroups at the European Network and Information Security Agency (ENISA) [4]) have identified that specifying security parameters in Service Level Agreements (termed as "Security Level Agreements" or SecLA over this paper) actually enables the establishment of a common semantic in order to model security among users and CSPs. However, despite the state of the art efforts aiming at building and representing Cloud SecLAs (e.g., the CSA's SLA and PLA working groups [1]), there is still a gap on the techniques to *reason* about them. In particular we refer to the techniques aimed to quantitatively evaluate the security level provided by the SecLA, this being a core requirement to enable the proposed negotiation of Cloud resources based on security parameters (just as presented in our previous research [5] and [6]).

This paper proposes a novel methodology and architecture to systematically broker Cloud resources based on *(i)* a technique to quantitatively evaluate and rank SecLAs and, *(ii)* a set of building blocks to enable the user-centric negotiation of Cloud security parameters. Our joint research contributes with a practical approach that extends the Cloud SecLA evaluation technique contributed by Luna [6], to enable the negotiation and brokerage of Cloud resources presented in [2] using the well-known WS-Agreement protocol [7].

The overall vision of this paper is represented in Fig. 1, where an iterative *Negotiation* process (Step 1) quantifies and ranks the user security requirements

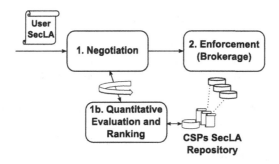

Fig. 1. Overview of the proposed security negotiation and brokerage of Cloud resources.

(i.e., represented as a *User SecLA*), with respect to one or more CSP SecLAs (Step 1b). Once an existing *CSP SecLA* offer matches the *User SecLA*, then an *Enforcement* stage takes place i.e., the broker acquires and delivers CSP resources to user (Step 2). This paper is focused on developing the details related with the underlying negotiation stage, whereas the resource brokering is out of scope. Notice that both the Negotiation (Step 1) and Evaluation (Step 1b) stages are not completely independent: security negotiation needs the quantitative evaluation of SecLA in order to rank the available CSP with respect to a user requirement, whereas the evaluation stage applies a user-defined negotiation criteria in order to classify the CSPs' security features.

This paper also proposes an architecture to implement the presented SecLA negotiation methodology in the context of a Cloud Federation, using the framework being developed by the EU FP7 mOSAIC project [8]. This framework enables the creation of distributed Cloud applications through a set of components based on the management and negotiation of Service Level Agreements.

Finally, to demonstrate the feasibility of our proposal we present the case study of a real system that implements the negotiation of a *User SecLA* with respect to a set of *CSPs SecLAs*, based on the information available in STAR [9] and the WS-Agreement standard [7].

The paper is organized as follows: Sect. 2 introduces the basic concepts behind the proposed security negotiation approach, Sect. 3 describes how Cloud SecLAs can be specified using WS-Agreement in order to enable its negotiation via the architecture presented in Sect. 4. A real case study that applies the proposed approach is discussed in Sect. 5, Sect. 6 analyzes related works and, finally Sect. 7 presents our conclusions.

2 Quantitatively Evaluating and Ranking Cloud SecLAs

Two base concepts driving our proposal are presented in this section. First, we discuss in further detail the notion of Cloud SecLAs (cf. Sect. 2.1). Second, in Sect. 2.2 are presented the basics of a technique to reason about SecLA, in particular to enable its quantitative evaluation as required by the negotiation process presented in this paper.

2.1 Cloud Security Level Agreements

The concept of SecLAs currently exists in varied dimensions and the Cloud is not an exception. The use of Cloud SecLAs has the potential to provide tangible benefits to CSPs especially associated with improved security administration and management practices, thus allowing for transparency to end users. Providing security related information in the form of Cloud SecLAs will undoubtedly result in enhanced security on CSP's side as the CSPs will at least have to think of the security aspects covered by the SecLA and will be forced to explicitly address some of them. The end users can also benefit from SecLAs by understanding the costs and benefits associated with this new service model. Also ENISA has recognized the significance of Cloud SecLAs in a recent study [4]. The results of the survey ENISA conducted show that the customers do not monitor the security aspects of their contracted SLAs on a continuous basis and in that way are unaware of the security of their services. This poses the risk that missing security measures can only become obvious after a security incident has happened. To address this problem the European Cloud computing strategy considers the development of template contracts and service level agreements (SLA) that do not only cover availability parameters, but also other security parameters e.g., related with confidentiality and integrity.

As introduced by Bernsmed [10], a Cloud SecLA usually models the CSP security at the *service level* using *Cloud SecLAs Templates* designed by multidisciplinary working groups (e.g., the Cloud Security Alliance's SLA and PLA work groups [1]). The templates can be derived from a set of expert-driven security requirements or based on a preliminary threat-analysis. The result is an organized collection of security statements (also called "security provisions") in the form {*security attribute, value*} (e.g., {*Backup Frequency, Daily*} and {*Encryption Key Size, 512 bits*}), as also proposed in different industrial and academic works [11–13] and [14]. In order to be manageable, these security provisions are usually organized into "hierarchical categories" derived from a taxonomy e.g., Savola [15] or the CSA's Consensus Assessment Initiative Questionnaire (CAIQ) [16]. Cloud SecLAs are usually stored in publicly available – and trusted – repositories like e.g., the CSA's "Security, Trust & Assurance Registry" [9]. Apart from the challenges related with the creation of SecLAs in real Cloud deployments, the current paucity of techniques to *quantitatively reason* about them has proven to be part of the obstacles in using SecLAs, just as mentioned by Almorsy [17] and [5]. In order to contribute towards bridging this gap, the next section presents the basics of a Cloud SecLA evaluation technique which will be used by the negotiation mechanism proposed later in this paper.

2.2 Quantitative SecLA Evaluation at a Glance

For the contributed negotiation process (cf., Step 1 in Fig. 1) it is helpful to have a user-centric mechanism to quantitatively evaluate and objectively rank SecLAs with respect to a predefined user requirement (Step 1b). Our approach extends the notion of Cloud SecLA benchmarking proposed in [6], through the use of quantitative rankings, as an enabler of the proposed negotiation process. The overall intent is to *(a)* systematically quantify the security level associated with each SecLA involved in the negotiation process (i.e., *User SecLA* and *CSPs SecLA*) and *(b)* use the data from *(a)* to allow the systematic elicitation of the CSP that is closer to the user's security requirements. For the purposes of this paper, only three basic concepts of the SecLA evaluation are presented and the interested readers are referred to [6] for further details.

First Concept. A key consideration in this paper is that SecLAs have a twofold use: on one hand, the authors make the realistic assumption (cf., Sect. 2.1) that each CSP is associated with a *CSP SecLA*, on the other hand, they also advocate for the use of SecLAs to represent security requirements of Cloud users thus *establishing a common semantic with CSPs for reasoning about security*. The proposed methodology relies on the assumption that each participating party (both end users and CSPs) elicit their security requirements using the same SecLA Template given as input in the methodology. The intuition behind this is that the use of different templates for security evaluation and ranking would be less practical.

User-defined requirements (termed as *User SecLA*) are a distinctive element of Cloud SecLA, where all the security provisions are *weighted* in order to represent their relative importance from user's perspective (e.g., for some users "Encryption Key Size" might be more important than "Backup Frequency"). Furthermore, for the sake of usability the technique proposed in [6] also considers that either quantitative weights (e.g., from 0 to 1) or qualitative weights (e.g., low/medium/high) can be assigned at different levels of the *User SecLA*. Important to be noticed is that there are specific rules that have to be considered when setting the weights to the individual security provisions. The sum of the weights associated with a set of sibling security provisions (e.g., those having the same parent category) must be equal to 1. Moreover, the user can choose only specific security provisions to rank by setting the weights to all the provisions not of interest to 0. A convenient approach for assigning the weights is to associate all the security provisions in a set of siblings with the same weights at the beginning. Then the important provisions have to be identified and their weights can be increased at the expense of the weights of the less important security provisions. Apart from the weights, we propose incorporating AND/OR relationships between the different categories within a SecLA Template. The aim of the AND relationships is to model hard-requirements, while the OR relationships aim to model soft-requirements. The intuition behind it is that if three properties are required for achieving a security goal, they exhibit an AND relationship, but if only one of them suffices for achieving the goal, an OR relationship is present.

Second Concept. The second concept is a mapping process that allows representing any Cloud SecLA (usually these documents are informally formatted) as a data structure that can be systematically processed. This step is needed to enable both humans and computers to quantitatively reason about the SecLAs overcoming the limitations stemming from their informal representation. These data structures (called "Quantitative Policy Trees" or QPT in [6]), are an

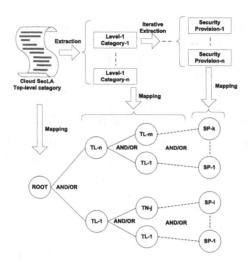

Fig. 2. SecLA-to-QPT: mapping a Cloud SecLA into a QPT [6].

extended version of classical "AND-OR" trees used to integrate both security requirements and associated quantifiers needed by the quantitative evaluation process. For the purposes of this paper and due to space restrictions, only a high-level view of the process to map SecLAs to QPT is presented in Fig. 2. The outcomes of the mapping process are *(i)* a *User QPT* populated with the weights and security provisions' values specified in the *User SecLA* and, *(ii)* one or more *CSP QPTs* mapped from its respective *CSP SecLAs* and also populated with the corresponding security provisions' values.

Third Concept. The third and final concept required from [6] is a set of rules to quantitatively aggregate and propagate the weights and security provision's values (also known as Local Security Levels or LSL) to the whole QPT (i.e., from leaf nodes up to the root node). Once the *User QPT* and the *CSP QPTs* have been populated with the aggregated values, it is possible to apply a ranking algorithm to determine how different CSPs under-/over-provision user's requirements. In [6] are proposed two different ranking techniques: a quantitative ranking (e.g., a real number on the interval $\{0 \dots 1\}$) that due to its nature is more suitable for automated systems than for humans and, a qualitative ranking that aims to be more "human-friendly" by using a set of qualitative labels (e.g., { *"Copper"*, *"Silver"*, *"Gold"*}) to represent the QPT evaluation's results.

The proposed quantitative aggregation methodology takes as input the User QPT and the CSP QPT along with the values associated with their security attributes at the leaf nodes. The aggregation rules that have to be applied for the propagation of the security values up to the QPT's root are defined by the proposed methodology and depend on the relationships between the siblings within the nodes. Within an AND node, the aggregated security level depends on all the sibling nodes, whereas within an OR node the "weakest-link" security principle is followed, and the aggregated security level is determined only by the

Listing 1.1. SDT element in WS-Agreement.

```
<wsag:ServiceDescriptionTerm wsag:Name="
    CustomerAccessRequirements"
wsag:ServiceName="SecurityArchitecture">

</wsag:ServiceDescriptionTerm>
```

sibling node with the smallest security level. The use of weights guarantees that the security provisions will contribute to the overall security level as defined by the end user. Once the QPTs have been populated with the aggregated values, it is possible to apply a ranking algorithm to determine how different CSPs underprovision or overprovision user's requirements. In the rest of this paper, we will show that the previously presented notion of quantitative ranks can be extended to actually negotiate Cloud resources using a broker-based architecture.

3 Creating and Specifying SecLAs Using WS-Agreement

As introduced in Sect. 1, the goal of the proposed approach is to offer the systematic negotiation of security using Cloud SecLAs. In order to fulfill this goal our proposal *(i)* creates a set of *CSP SecLAs* based on the security information derived from the CSA STAR repository [9] and, *(ii)* represents both *CSP/User SecLAs* using the WS-Agreement standard [7]. In this section we discuss in further detail these two phases.

First, given CSA STAR's broad adoption by major CSPs our research proposes the creation of SecLAs derived from the information stored there. Currently, STAR contains entries in the form of "Consensus Assessments Initiative Questionnaire" reports (CAIQ [16]), which provide industry-accepted ways to document what security controls exist in Cloud offerings. The current CAIQ report contains a set of 171 security parameters (all of these with a qualitative "YES/NO" answer) distributed in the following *controls*: Compliance (CO) – 14, Data Governance (DG) – 15, Facility Security (FS) – 9, Human Resources Security (HR) – 4, Information Security (IS) – 71, Legal (LG) – 2, Operations Management (OP) – 5, Risk Management (RI) – 12, Release Management (RM) – 5, Resilience (RS) – 11 and Security Architecture (SA) – 23. Given these CAIQ's properties, it is possible to create SecLAs with the features required by the evaluation and ranking methodology presented in Sect. 2.

Second, to allow the systematic negotiation of Cloud SecLAs (derived from the CAIQ as mentioned in the previous paragraph), we adopted the SLA-oriented language proposed by WS-Agreement which was created with the goal to standardize the terminology/protocol used when two parties are trying to establish an agreement. It mainly consists of a language for specifying the nature of the agreement and, a SOAP-based protocol for actually establishing the agreement between two participants. At state of art, the WS-Agreement language is widely used for SLA negotiation and has been adopted by projects like EU FP7 mOSAIC [8].

The main component within the WS-Agreement standard is the *SLA specification core*, which consists of three elements: *Service Description Terms (SDT)*, *Service Properties (SP) and, Guarantee Terms (GT)*. A SDT is a fundamental element, providing a full or partial functional description of a service. One or more SDTs can be related to a service. A SP element defines properties/variables, associated with a service, and used for expressing guarantees on a service. Finally, a GT element defines an assurance on a service through an assertion (using the content of the SP element) expressed over the service described by the SDTs. In the rest of this section we present the process required to specify a SecLA using the WS-Agreement standard, however due to space restrictions our explanation will only show relevant excerpts of the resulting XML document.

Based on the CAIQ's structure [16], first we model each security control as a SDT. Then, the respective value of the controls along with the inputs required by the evaluation technique presented in Sect. 2 (i.e., the *User SecLA's* AND/OR relationships and weights) are modeled as GTs on the SDT. CAIQ's inherent hierarchical structure (i.e., sub-controls) is represented as security elements in WS-Agreement (cf., Listing 1.1).

Listing 1.2. SP element in WS-Agreement.

```
<wsag:ServiceProperties wsag:Name="
    CustomerAccessRequirements"
wsag:ServiceName="SecurityArchitecture">
 <wsag:VariableSet>
  <wsag:Variable wsag:Name="SA-01.1"wsag:Metric="boolean"
     >
    <wsag:Location>$this/wsag:Terms/wsag:All/
       wsag:ServiceDescriptionTerm
    [@wsag:Name ='CustomerAccessRequirements']</
       wsag:Location>
  </wsag:Variable>
  <wsag:Variable wsag:Name="SA-01.Q1"wsag:Metric="string"
     >
    <wsag:Location>$this/wsag:Terms/wsag:All/
       wsag:ServiceDescriptionTerm
    [@wsag:Name ='CustomerAccessRequirements']</
       wsag:Location>
  </wsag:Variable>
  <wsag:Variable wsag:Name="Weight"wsag:Metric="float">
    <wsag:Location>$this/wsag:Terms/wsag:All/
       wsag:ServiceDescriptionTerm
    [@wsag:Name ='CustomerAccessRequirements']</
       wsag:Location>
  </wsag:Variable>
 </wsag:VariableSet>
</wsag:ServiceProperties>
```

Once the SDT has been specified, we have to focus on the SP element. First, we define a SP for each CAIQ sub-control, as required by its respective SDT (cf., Listing 1.2). Second, in the SP element we define the variables (e.g., weights) and related semantics used for expressing the security requirements through assertions in the GT element.

For the GT description, the user can define a guarantee on a security service expressed as an assertion in the Service Level Objective (SLO). The data required to model this assertion are: the security level of the CAIQ control, the AND/OR relationships and the weights. A more detailed explanation of the GT element will be presented in Sect. 5.

Up to this point, we have fully developed the structure of an empty WS-Agreement template "compliant" with the Cloud SecLA evaluation technique summarized in Sect. 2. Both users and CSPs are now able to populate this template with their own security controls and values, so the final set of SecLA documents can be used for negotiation purposes just as presented in the following section.

4 An Architectural Model for a SecLA-Based Cloud Brokering

The above illustrated evaluation methodology provides a theoretical basis for evaluating and comparing SecLAs. In this section, we present an example Cloud application that relies on such techniques to provide a security-oriented brokering functionality. In particular, we focus on an application offering security-oriented Cloud federation of IaaS resources: such example, which will be further developed in the context of the SPECS project, clearly demonstrates the needs of evaluation techniques as the ones presented above.

A Cloud federation consists in multiple external and internal Cloud computing services, deployed and jointly managed with the aim of matching specific business needs. The set-up of a Cloud federation could be subject to security requirements: as an example, let us consider the case of a Cloud user that needs to evaluate the security provided by different CSPs, in order to decide which one better suits her requirements. At the state of the art, when using the resources of a Cloud federation, users have to manually manage their security requirements (e.g., choose a provider based on their existing ISO2700 certifications) and, in many cases, they do not have the means to actually monitor if these requirements are being fulfilled by the involved CSPs.

By adopting an approach based on SecLAs instead, it is possible for the users to understand what the Cloud is able to guarantee in terms of security, and this information can be used to take informed decisions about the CSP to contact. It is important to point out however, that the user still needs proper tools to systematically reason about SecLAs, including side-by-side CSP comparison, negotiation and continuous monitoring.

In order to address these issues, we propose an innovative brokering solution in which:

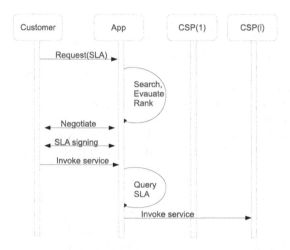

Fig. 3. Application behaviour (Updated picture).

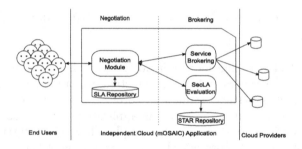

Fig. 4. Proposed SecLA negotiation architecture.

– Cloud security parameters can be specified in the form of SecLAs.
– a Security-as-a-Service broker can be deployed between users and various Clouds or even Cloud Federations to automatically manage the whole SecLA life-cycle.

The behavior we aim at obtaining is illustrated in Fig. 3, where the *App* box represents the introduced brokering system. With respect to ETSI CSCC Terminology [18], the Cloud application we are proposing is a Cloud Provider that offers a service (the brokering) to users, consisting in the invocation, on their behalf, of external Cloud (IaaS) services on the basis of a negotiated SecLA.

Figure 3 shows how a user can use the *App* services in order to negotiate security parameters related to a given service. First of all, we assume that the application locally stores signed SecLAs that express the security guarantees given by a set of CSPs to the users. When the user submits her request in terms of desired parameters, the Application checks what has been previously agreed upon by accessing the local signed SecLAs and, consequently, invokes the

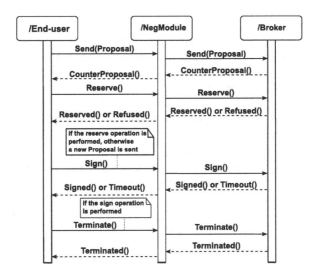

Fig. 5. User-centric Cloud SecLA Negotiation Protocol.

provider that grants such features. The SecLA negotiation (which is actually a guided selection of remote CSPs) is based on the quantitative evaluation of the offerings from different providers.

4.1   Application Design

In order to meet the requirements above described, we propose the three-tier architecture shown in Fig. 4, where the intermediate layer is composed of the following modules: *(i)* the *Negotiation module*, which has the role of managing the interactions with end users, *(ii)* the *SecLA Evaluation module*, which implements the technique presented in Sect. 2.2, and *(ii)* the *Service Brokering module*, in charge of brokering the elicited Cloud services. In this section we will focus on the Negotiation and SecLA Evaluation modules, but interested readers can refer to Rak [2, 19] for a full description of SLA management using an user-centric approach.

4.2   The User-Centric Negotiation Protocol

The Negotiation module interacts with users in order to identify their requirements (i.e., create an *User SecLA*), and applies the results of the quantitative SecLA evaluation/ranking (cf., Sect. 2.2) in order to orchestrate the overall negotiation process. We assume that users are able to specify their security requirements in the form of a *User SecLA* (even if they are not security experts), using the CSA CAIQ reports [16] as a guidance. As mentioned in Sect. 3, the STAR repository [9] can be used as a *trusted* source for creating *CSPs SecLAs*. The Cloud SecLA negotiation protocol shown in Fig. 5 is the user-centric mechanism we propose to allow end users and CSPs to arrive to an agreement on the requested/provided security levels.

The proposed protocol works as follows: once the user has created a *User SecLA* with his specific security requirements, the negotiation process starts by submitting it to the Negotiation module. Upon reception, the Negotiation module forwards the *User SecLA* to the SecLA Evaluation module, which implements the technique described in Sect. 2.2 to quantitatively evaluate and rank the user requirements with respect to a set of available *CSPs SecLAs* (previously fetched from a repository like STAR). As a result, the SecLA Evaluation module returns to the user this set of CSPs, but ordered with respect to the requested *User SecLA* (e.g., quantitatively ranked from best to worst). In this case the user is given the chance to make (either automatically or manually) an informed decision by choosing a CSP from this resulting set.

The user-selected *CSP SecLA* is then submitted to the Broker, so it can be either reserved or refused. If the selection is refused, then the user has to submit a new proposal (i.e., another CSP SecLA), otherwise a *timeout* is set for the *CSP SecLA*, being the maximum period of time that can elapse before a user finally agrees on the reserved CSP. When the user decides to continue with the resource reservation, an agreement can be signed and the negotiation process can be terminated.

The negotiation protocol presented in this subsection can be deployed using both the SLA Framework developed in [20] and, the WS-Agreement standard. Although those implementation details are out of the scope of this paper, in the next section we show the feasibility of the proposed approach with a real case study.

5   Case Study: Negotiating CAIQ-Based Security

In order to demonstrate how the proposed negotiation mechanism can be used with real-world information, in this section we present a case study that uses the CSP data stored in CSA STAR [9], a publicly available repository that documents the security controls provided by CSPs worldwide. We show that our user-centric negotiation mechanism can use STAR data *(i)* to establish a common semantic with respect to the security offered by the CSP and, *(ii)* to enable Cloud customers automatically choose the CSP that better fulfills their security requirements. As mentioned in Sect. 3, the STAR repository contains only *static* security controls (i.e., not updated in real-time by the CSP), however the proposed negotiation approach can be easily extended to manage real-time information e.g., generated by continuous security monitoring systems (cf., Sect. 7).

The main goal of this case study is to show the feasibility of our approach, so it has been simplified with respect to the information (i.e., number of STAR's security controls) being used. Nevertheless, the base negotiation techniques can be applied to more complex real-world case studies as the use cases presented in the FP7 SPECS [21]. In one of the SPECS' scenarios the user wants to use Infrastructure as a Service (IaaS) from a Cloud Federation and has some specific security requirements that can be expressed in the form of SecLA. They have to be fulfilled and observed during the whole usage period. In this case the proposed methodology can be applied in the process of finding the CSP that best fulfills

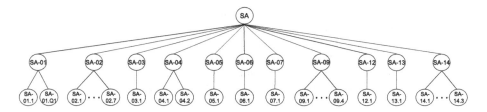

Fig. 6. SecLA tree for the Security Architecture (SA) category of the CAIQ reports [16].

user's demands considering the whole supply chain. Another SPECS-related use case for the proposed methodology is given by a customer who wants to store data on a remote Cloud Provider [21]. The customer has specific confidentiality requirements that can be given in the form of a SecLA. The respective CSPs that can provide the requested service can be evaluated and ranked taking into account user's requirements using the approach proposed in this paper.

For simplicity reasons, in this section we also assume that a user only wants to specify in her *User SecLA* some specific requirements, mostly related to the security mechanisms implemented by the CSP. Using the CAIQ terminology [16], this user requirement translates to an *User SecLA* containing only the parameters under the Security Architecture (SA) control (cf., Fig. 6).

As mentioned in Sect. 3, the user expresses her security requirements as a WS-Agreement document that is, in terms of both service and guarantee terms (cf. Section 3). More specifically, the user can define a GT over a particular service in the form of an assertion in the SLO element. This is the basis for applying the negotiation process described in Sect. 4. It should be noticed that the GT element, the CAIQ and the QPT (cf., Sect. 2) have the same hierarchical structure, therefore the user can specify her requirements with different levels of granularity. For example, she can define a minimum requirement at the "root" SA control, but also at each one of its "leaf" sub-controls (e.g., SA-01, SA-01.Q1, ...) just as shown in Listings 1.3 and 1.4. Furthermore, these excerpts of the WS-Agreement document also show that numeric weights can be assigned to individual controls, in order to represent its relative importance from a user perspective.

Tables 1 and 2 show the quantitative results of the negotiation process, after applying the evaluation technique (cf., Sect. 2.2) to the following set of Cloud SecLAs:

- Three well-known CSPs (i.e., *CSP1* to *CSP3*) taken from the CSA STAR repository[1].
- Two different user requirements with the same relative weights per-SA control. The first one ($User_{min}$) using the minimum allowable Local Security Levels or LSL (i.e., LSL = 1), whereas the second one ($User_{max}$) using the maximum

---

[1] Due to STAR's usage restrictions, it is not possible to disclose the real identity of the CSPs under evaluation.

Listing 1.3. A Guarantee Term element in WS-Agreement.

```
<wsag:GuaranteeTerm wsag:Name="
    UserRequirementOnCustomerAccess"
Obligated="Provider">
  <wsag:ServiceScope ServiceName="string">
      SecurityArchitecture</wsag:ServiceScope>

  <wsag:ServiceLevelObjective>
    <wsag:CustomServiceLevel>
    (SA-01.1 EQ true, Weight EQ 0.5) AND (SA-01.Q1 EQ
        SLA, Weight EQ 0.5)
    </wsag:CustomServiceLevel>
  </wsag:ServiceLevelObjective>

  <wsag:BusinessValueList>
    .....
  </wsag:BusinessValueList>
</wsag:GuaranteeTerm>
```

Listing 1.4. A Guarantee Term element in WS-Agreement.

```
<wsag:GuaranteeTerm wsag:Name="
    UserRequirementOnSecurityArch"Obligated="Provider">
  <wsag:ServiceScope ServiceName="string">
      SecurityArchitecture</wsag:ServiceScope>

  <wsag:ServiceLevelObjective>
    <wsag:CustomServiceLevel>
    (CustomerAccessRequirements EQ 0.4, Weight EQ 0.5)
    AND (UserIDCredentials EQ 0.4, Weight EQ 0.5)
    AND (DataSecurityIntegrity EQ 0.4, Weight EQ 0.5)
    AND (ApplicationSecurity EQ 0.4, Weight EQ 0.5)
    AND (DataIntegrity EQ 0.4, Weight EQ 0.5)
    AND (ProductionEnvironments EQ 0.4, Weight EQ 0.5)
    AND (RemoteUserMultifactorAuth EQ 0.4, Weight EQ 0.5)
    AND (Segmentation EQ 0.4, Weight EQ 0.5)
    AND (ClockSynchronization EQ 0.4, Weight EQ 0.5)
    AND (EquipmentIndentification EQ 0.4, Weight EQ 0.5)
    AND (AuditLoggingIntrusionDetection EQ 0.4, Weight EQ
        0.5)
    </wsag:CustomServiceLevel>
  </wsag:ServiceLevelObjective>

  <wsag:BusinessValueList>
    .....
  </wsag:BusinessValueList>
</wsag:GuaranteeTerm>
```

Table 1. Quantitative evaluation of the $User_{min}$ SecLA requirement.

	CSP_1	CSP_2	CSP_3
SA Aggregated	2.86	2.16	2.6
SA-01	1.50	3.00	2.50
SA-02	3.00	1.29	2.14
SA-03	3.00	3.00	3.00
SA-04	3.00	1.50	3.00
SA-05	3.00	3.00	3.00
SA-06	3.00	0	3.00
SA-07	3.00	3.00	0
SA-09	3.00	3.00	3.00
SA-12	3.00	3.00	3.00
SA-13	3.00	0	3.00
SA-14	3.00	3.00	3.00

Table 2. Quantitative evaluation of the $User_{max}$ SecLA requirement.

	CSP_1	CSP_2	CSP_3
SA Aggregated	−0.14	−0.84	−0.4
SA-01	−1.50	0	−0.50
SA-02	0	−1.71	−0.86
SA-03	0	0	0
SA-04	0	−1.50	0
SA-05	0	0	0
SA-06	0	−3.00	0
SA-07	0	0	−3.00
SA-09	0	0	0
SA-12	0	0	0
SA-13	0	−3.00	0
SA-14	0	0	0

(i.e., LSL = 4). Notice that three SA-controls (i.e., SA-08, SA-10, SA-11) are not shown in the results, because they did not apply to the evaluated CSPs.

Obtained results in Tables 1 and 2, show that at the *SA Aggregated* level the contributed negotiation methodology allows ranking the available CSPs as $\{CSP_2, CSP_3, CSP_1\}$ for $User_{min}$, but as $\{CSP_1, CSP_3, CSP_2\}$ for $User_{max}$. As a rule of thumb, the more appropriate CSP (i.e., the one that best fulfills the user requirement) will be the one with the quantitative score closest to zero (i.e., the *User SecLA* baseline). Finally, the resulting set of ranked CSPs is returned to user, so she can either *(i)* *automatically* decide the one to use (i.e., the best ranked) or, *(ii)* *manually* apply additional criteria for the decision making process (e.g., CSP price). Future research will also focus on the evaluation of non-security related parameters, which might be taken into account to perform a more comprehensive negotiation process.

6   Related Work

To the best of our knowledge, there are only two previous works related with the idea proposed in this paper for Cloud ecosystems. The first one was contributed by Rak [22], where authentication and authorization mechanisms are negotiated between users and CSPs via a SLA-based interface in the context of the EU FP7 mOSAIC project [8]. Our research improves over the ideas described in [22], by contributing with a common semantic (the Cloud SecLA) and an evaluation technique to quantitatively match the user's security requirements with respect to a set of available CSP. In the second related work Hale [23] introduced SecAgreements, a framework for negotiating Cloud security risks via *(i)* a SLA-based matchmaking algorithm and, *(ii)* a set of extensions proposed for the WS-Agreement protocol [7]. Despite the similarities with our research, on one hand SecAgreements' matchmaking algorithm is not user-centric and only can specify weights at the individual security provision-level, thus lacking of the usability offered by our evaluation approach (cf., Sect. 2.2). On the other hand, as future work we are planning to research if the risk-based approach proposed by SecAgreements [23] might be used to complement our own negotiation methodology.

7   Conclusions

In this paper we have introduced the foundations for negotiating and brokering Cloud resources based on the notion of Security Level Agreements. At the core of the negotiation stage is a user-centric technique for quantitatively evaluating and ranking SecLAs, being developed within the EU FP7 ABC4Trust project [24]. Through the notion of Cloud SecLAs, our quantitative evaluation technique offers a common semantic to systematically match a *User SecLA* requirement with respect to the most appropriate CSP. Based on our experience within the EU FP7 mOSAIC project [8], this paper also presented an architecture and protocol to implement the proposed Cloud negotiation mechanism. The feasibility of the proposed approach was demonstrated through a real-world case study that used the CSP information contained in the CSA STAR repository [9].

Despite STAR contains only static/declarative information about CSPs, our negotiation approach has the potential to use also "dynamic" security data (e.g., measured in real-time by network sensors), directly embedded into the WS-Agreement protocol. We have also shown that the contributed methodology is suitable for Cloud Federations, where the negotiation of security parameters is a critical factor taking into account the amount of available CSP.

Once the envisioned architecture is deployed using the mOSAIC framework [8], future work will empirically analyze in detail the technical trade-offs (e.g., from the performance perspective) between SLA-based resource negotiation and, the SecLA-based mechanism presented in this paper. Finally, future activities will also research "advanced" negotiation features not considered so far e.g., re-negotiation and continuous monitoring.

Acknowledgements. Research supported in part by the Deutsche Forschungsgemein-schaft (German Research Foundation) Graduiertenkolleg 1362 - DFG GRK 1362, the EC FP7 project SPECS (Grant Agreement no. 610795), the FP7-ICT-2009-5-256910 (mOSAIC) and TU Darmstadt's project LOEWE-CASED.

References

1. Cloud Security Alliance: Security and Privacy Level Agreements working groups (2012). https://cloudsecurityalliance.org/research/pla/. Accessed on 10.01.14
2. Rak, M., Aversa, R., Venticinque, S., Di Martino, B.: User centric service level management in mOSAIC applications. In: Alexander, M., et al. (eds.) Euro-Par 2011, Part II. LNCS, vol. 7156, pp. 106–115. Springer, Heidelberg (2012)
3. Kandukuri, B.R., et. al.: Cloud security issues. In: Proceedings of the IEEE International Conference on Services Computing, pp. 517–520. IEEE, New York (2009)
4. Dekker, M., Hogben, G.: Survey and analysis of security parameters in cloud SLAs across the European public sector. Technical report TR-2011-12-19, European Network and Information Security Agency (2011)
5. Luna, J., et al.: Quantitative assessment of cloud security level agreements: a case study. In: Samarati, P., Lou, W., Zhou, J. (eds.) Proceedings of Security and Cryptography, pp. 64–73. SciTePress (2012)
6. Luna, J., et al.: Benchmarking cloud security level agreements using quantitative policy trees. In: Proceedings of the 2012 ACM Workshop on Cloud Computing Security Workshop, CCSW '12, pp. 103–112. ACM, New York (2012)
7. Andrieux, K., et al.: Web services agreement specification (WS-Agreement). Technical report TR-WSAgreement-2007, Open Grid Forum (2007)
8. mOSAIC: mOSAIC FP7 (2011). http://www.mosaic-cloud.eu/. Accessed on 05.10.13
9. Cloud Security Alliance: The Security, Trust & Assurance Registry (STAR) (2011). https://cloudsecurityalliance.org/star/. Accessed on 10.01.14
10. Bernsmed, K., et al.: Security SLAs for federated cloud services. In: Proceedings of IEEE Availability, Reliability and Security, pp. 202–209. IEEE, New York (2011)
11. Casola, V., et al.: A SLA evaluation methodology in service oriented architectures. In: Gollmann, D., Massacci, F., Yautsiukhin, A. (eds.) Quality of Protection. Advances in Information Security, vol. 23, pp. 119–130. Springer, Berlin (2006)
12. Valentina, C., et al.: A reference model for security level evaluation: policy and fuzzy techniques. J. UCS **11**, 150–174 (2005)
13. Samani, R., et al.: Common assurance maturity model: scoring model (2011). http://common-assurance.com/. Accessed on 10.12.13
14. Luna, J., et al.: A security metrics framework for the cloud. In: Lopez, J., Samarati, P. (eds.) Proceedings of Security and Cryptography, pp. 245–250. SciTePress (2011)

15. Savola, R., et al.: Towards wider cloud service applicability by security, privacy and trust measurements. In: Proceedings of IEEE Application of Information and Communication Technologies, pp. 1–6. IEEE, New York (2010)
16. Cloud Security Alliance: The Consensus Assessments Initiative Questionnaire (2011). https://cloudsecurityalliance.org/research/cai/. Accessed on 14.01.14
17. Almorsy, M., et al.: Collaboration-based cloud computing security management framework. In: Proceedings of IEEE International Conference on Cloud Computing, pp. 364–371. IEEE, New York (2011)
18. ETSI: Cloud Standards Coordination (2013). Accessed on 12.11.13.
19. Rak, M., Ficco, M.: Intrusion tolerance as a service - a SLA-based solution. In: Leymann, F., Ivanov, I., van Sinderen, M., Shan, T. (eds.): Proceedings of the International Conference on Cloud Computing and Services Science (CLOSER), pp. 375–384, SciTePress (2012)
20. Amato, A., et. al.: SLA negotiation and brokering for sky computing. In: Leymann, F., Ivanov, I., van Sinderen, M., Shan, T. (eds).: In: Proceedings of the International Conference on Cloud Computing and Services Science (CLOSER), pp. 611–620. SciTePress (2012)
21. SPECS: SPECS FP7 (2013). http://www.specs-project.eu/. Accessed on 14.01.14
22. Rak, M., et. al.: A SLA-based interface for security management in cloud and GRID integrations. In: Proceedings of the IEEE International Conference on Information Assurance and Security, pp. 378–383. IEEE, New York (2011)
23. Hale, M.L., Gamble R.: SecAgreement: advancing security risk calculations in cloud services. In: Proceedings of the IEEE World Congress on Services, pp. 133–140. IEEE , New York (2012)
24. ABC4Trust: ABC4Trust FP7 (2011). http://www.abc4trust.eu/. Accessed on 14.12.13

Trustworthiness Attributes and Metrics for Engineering Trusted Internet-Based Software Systems

Nazila Gol Mohammadi[1]([⊠]), Sachar Paulus[2], Mohamed Bishr[1],
Andreas Metzger[1], Holger Könnecke[2], Sandro Hartenstein[2],
Thorsten Weyer[1], and Klaus Pohl[1]

[1] Paluno – The Ruhr Institute for Software Technology,
Duisburg-Essen University, 45127 Essen, Germany
{nazila.golmohammadi,mohamed.bishr,andreas.metzger,
thorsten.weyer,klaus.pohl}@paluno.uni-due.de
[2] Department of Economics, Brandenburg University of Applied Sciences,
14770 Brandenburg, Germany
{sachar.paulus,holger.koennecke,
sandro.hartenstein}@fh-brandenburg.de

Abstract. Trustworthiness of Internet-based software systems, apps, services and platform is a key success factor for their use and acceptance by organizations and end-users. The notion of trustworthiness, though, is subject to individual interpretation and preference, e.g., organizations require confidence about how their business critical data is handled whereas end-users may be more concerned about usability. As one main contribution, we present an extensive list of software quality attributes that contribute to trustworthiness. Those software quality attributes have been identified by a systematic review of the research literature and by analyzing two real-world use cases. As a second contribution, we sketch an approach for systematically deriving metrics to measure the trustworthiness of software system. Our work thereby contributes to better understanding which software quality attributes should be considered and assured when engineering trustworthy Internet-based software systems.

Keywords: Trust · Trustworthiness · Trustworthiness attributes · Socio-Technical Systems · Information and communication technologies · Metric

1 Introduction

Trust underlies almost every social and economic relation and is regarded as the glue that binds society together. Humans, processes and organizations, with different perceptions and goals, increasingly interact via the Internet. In such online settings, gaining and establishing trust relations within socio-economic systems becomes more difficult where interactions are mediated by technology rather than face-to-face communication making it more difficult to infer trust through social clues. The question this paper deals with is about the software system attributes that can foster trustworthiness in and within Socio-Technical Systems (STS) mediated through online networks.

M. Helfert et al. (Eds.): CLOSER 2013, CCIS 453, pp. 19–35, 2014.
DOI: 10.1007/978-3-319-11561-0_2

STS are increasingly becoming part of our daily life in form of apps, Internet-based applications, cyber-physical systems, services, etc. The people involved in online businesses, though, have generally limited information about each other and about the STS supporting their online and offline transactions. There are several reports indicating an increasing number of victims of cyber-crime leading to massive deterioration of trustworthiness in current STS. Therefore, individuals and organizations are becoming more and more concerned about trusting and placing confidence on current STS and show interest in how to handle their business critical data. Consequently, trustworthiness of a software, app, service or platform becomes a key factor for their wider use and adoption by organizations and end-users.

There are limited contributions that approach the trust and trustworthiness issues described from angles other than security. However, security is not the only aspect of trustworthiness. Most existing approaches have assumed that one-dimensional properties of services lead to trustworthiness of such services, and even to trust in it by users, such as a certification (e.g., Common Criteria), the presence of certain technologies (encryption), or the use of certain methodologies (SSE-CMM) [1–3]. In this work, we relax the assumptions of such a one-dimensional approach and instead consider a multitude of attributes.

With a literature review, we attempt to identify and capture the attributes so far known as contributing to trustworthiness. These attributes have been classified to major quality categories. This paper provides a structured and comprehensive overview on SQA and their contribution to trustworthiness. In addition, we provide methods for deriving trustworthiness metrics, which is also considered an important extension to our previous work in [28].

The remainder of this paper is structured as follows: Sect. 2 provides a brief overview on the fundamentals on trust and trustworthiness of STS. Section 3 discusses related work. Section 4 describes the classification of SQA contributing to trustworthiness and capture them as trustworthiness attributes. In Sect. 4.13 we finalized the introduced trustworthiness attributes with some recommendations. Section 5 investigates the existing methods for deriving metrics and presents our proposed method for defining trustworthiness metrics for evaluation of trustworthiness attributes. Section 6 presents our conclusions and the future work.

2 Fundamentals

This section introduces the notion of trust from different perspectives and moves on to define the meaning of trustworthiness and its relation to trust. We then identify the relation between trust and trustworthiness. Finally, we discuss how they relate to STS.

2.1 Trust and Trustworthiness: A Discussion

From a sociological perspective two converging branches of sociology characterize the field of STS. The first branch focuses on the societal whole, its complex structures and social systems. The second branch focuses on societal members, individual actions and relations between them. This second branch brought to attention trust as an element emerging from individual interactions and based on individual actions [4]. In this second branch, individuals rely on people engaged in representative activities [5], in other words, they rely on those who act on our behalf in matters of economy, politics, government and science. Such dependence implies high degrees of trust on part of the individual. Extending this view to information systems, we also rely on systems to run daily activities across large swaths of our society. They can be referred to as STS which are comprised of networks of individuals and IS organized around certain tasks. The delegation of tasks to such STS by individuals or organizations entails establishing some level of trust in such systems by the individuals. Consequently, it can be said that the trustworthiness of such systems is a key concern that needs to be fostered and even engineered in the fabric of these systems to maintain high levels of trust within society.

One of the problems occurring when studying a notion like trust is that everyone experiences trust. Hence, it is a personal view of what trust actually is [6]. This is the first intuitive explanation of why trust has multiple and varying definitions. A second explanation is the fact that there are multiple definitions of trust simply because there are many different types of trust [7, 8].

In [4] trust is defined as "a bet about the future contingent actions of others". The components of this definition are belief and commitment. There is a belief that placing trust in a person or a system will lead to a good outcome and then a commitment to actually place trust and take an action to use this system based on this belief. E.g., when a user decides to use a system on the web, then he is confident that it will meet his expectations. In [9], a different outlook on trust is presented by Luhmann. He explains that "further increases in complexity call for new mechanisms for the reduction of complexity". Luhmann suggests that trust is a more effective mechanism for this purpose. Given this view we can assert that increasing trust in STS has the effect of reducing uncertainty and complexity both online and offline in our society and this in turn has positive social and economic impacts.

In this paper, we stick to the earlier mentioned definition of trust in [4] while extending it to include STS: "a bet about the future contingent actions of others be they individuals or groups of individuals, or entire STS".

Trustworthiness on the other hand has been used sometimes as a synonym for security and sometimes for dependability. Trustworthiness in general is a broad-spectrum term with notions including reliability, security, performance, and user experience as parts of trustworthiness [10].

However, given our chosen definition of trust we argue that while trust is a concern that emerges from the personal observation of an STS by individuals, trustworthiness is a characteristic of the system that has the potential to influence the trust this person has in the system in a positive or negative way.

2.2 Trustworthiness in Socio-Technical Systems

STS are systems that include humans, organization and their IS. There are interactions between these autonomous participants, between human and organizations as a social and software system as technical interactions [11]. These social and technical components strongly influence each other. Our focus is on distributed applications that enable connection and communication of people via the Internet. Therefore, here, STS are applications, services, and platforms where technology and human behaviour are mutually dependent [12]. Thus, in STS people or organizations may communicate or collaborate with other people and organizations that emanate from interactions mediated by technology rather than face-to-face communication or collaboration [13].

STS are to be made trustworthy to merit the trust of their users. Trustworthiness has been defined as assurance that the system will perform as expected [14]. Furthermore, trustworthiness of software has been defined as worthy of being trusted to fulfil requirements which may be needed for a particular software component, application, system [15]. Trustworthiness is a potentially central aspect of distributed STS. We argue it as a multi-dimensional construct combining specific attributes, properties and characteristics.

The relation between trust and trustworthiness concepts always depends on reasoning processes which are performed by users of the system explicitly or implicitly considering the risk and possible consequences. There could be an imbalance between the level of trust in and the trustworthiness of the system with the possibility of two extreme cases. Typical situations are e.g., when too conservative users miss potential benefits of the system or when too optimistic users take too much risk by using the system (data misuse, etc.). Hence, there are major concerns about the trustworthiness of STS as the underestimation of side-effects of untrustworthy systems and mismanaging the vital and critical trust requirements has led to cyber-crime, e-frauds, cyber-terrorism, and sabotage. Reports [12] show an increased number of citizens that have fallen victim to these crimes, e.g., data loss. All of these issues occur because of either lack of trustworthiness or the awareness thereof.

Therefore, trustworthiness has recently gained increasing attention in public discussion. Figure 1 illustrates the identified gap in research in building a well-accepted STS for supporting socio-economic systems in the real world. The supporting applications lack expected (demonstrated) characteristics of such kinds of systems in the real world. The first step in closing this gap thus is the identification of trustworthiness attributes that may contribute to trust of socio-economic entities. Then, STS should be made capable to present these properties and characteristics.

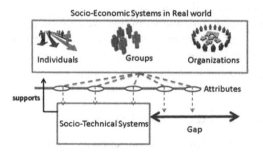

Fig. 1. The Socio-Technical gap inspired from [13].

There are, though, some inconsistencies between expected trust properties by the service consumer and promised trustworthiness from the service provider in general. To mitigate these deficiencies and to bridge the gap resulting from the asymmetry between trust and trustworthiness, we will investigate which trustworthiness attributes a system can hold (with which mechanism and/or technologies), and whether these attributes are capable of contributing to trustworthiness addressing the trust concerns of user.

3 Related Work

Trustworthiness in the literature has addressed the confidentiality of sensitive information, the integrity of valuable information, the prevention of unauthorized use of information, guaranteed QoS, the availability of critical data, reliability and integrity of infrastructure, the prevention of unauthorised use of infrastructure, etc. In order to prove being trustworthy, software applications could promise to cover a set of various quality attributes [10] depending on their domain and target users. Trustworthiness should promise a wide spectrum including reliability, security, performance, and user experience. But, Trustworthiness is domain and application dependent and a relative attribute, i.e. if a system was trustworthy in respect to some quality attribute like performance, it would not necessarily be successful in being secure. Trustworthiness and trust should not be regarded as a single construct with a single effect; rather it is strongly context dependent.

Related to this observation is the fact that the demonstration of trustworthiness attributes like Common Criteria certifications (ISO 15408) [16] or remote attestation procedures focus on security related attributes, whereas much more domains actually contribute to trustworthiness. E.g., a broad range of literature has argued and emphasized the relation between QoS and trustworthiness [17–22]. Therefore, trustworthiness is influenced by a number of quality attributes than just security-related. Trustworthiness of entities and individuals has been investigated in open, distributed systems (e.g., online marketplaces, multi agent systems, and peer-to-peer systems). Note that in this paper we strictly adhere to the perspective of a to-be-constructed system, and therefore will ignore potential trustworthiness (or trust) attributes like reputation or similar representing other users feedback, since they will only be available when the system is in use.

4 Survey of Trustworthiness Attributes

In this work, we investigate the properties and attributes of a software system that contribute to trustworthiness. To this end, we built on the software quality reference model defined by S-Cube [23]. The S-Cube model is extensive and has considered several other models such as: presented by Boehm [24], Adrion, et al. [25], McCall, et al. [26], and ISO 9126-1 [27]. In this paper we have excluded two types of the S-Cube SQA from our analysis. Firstly, some of the attributes contributing to trustworthiness are not identified in our literature review. Hence they were excluded.

Secondly, some quality attributes, e.g., integrity, can be achieved, among other ways, through encryption. In this case we included the high level attribute (integrity) as a contributor to trustworthiness but did not include encryption on its own because it is encompassed by the higher level attribute. Both cases are further discussed in Sect. 4.13. Additionally, we have included attributes that have been studied in the literature in terms of trustworthiness. These attributes are marked with an asterisk (*) in Fig. 2. This study is an extensive literature review. We aimed on identifying, evaluating and interpreting all available research relevant to an SQA and their potential on contributing to trustworthiness. The diagram below (Fig. 3) shows the resulted papers and their distribution in classified quality categories. Contributing characteristics of software systems to trustworthiness are captured as trustworthiness attributes. These attributes and belonging quality category are discussed in the following sections. The detailed literature and surveyed papers can be found in [28] with an indication of the respective papers. Figure 2 outlines the result of this work.

Trustworthiness Attributes

Security	Compatibility	Configuration	Compliance	Cost	Data related	Dependability	Performance	Usability	Correctness*	Complexity*
Accountability	Openness*	related quality	Privacy*		quality	Accuracy	Throughput	Satisfaction		Composability
Auditability/	Reusability*	Stability			Data Integrity	Availability	Response Time	Learnability		
Traceability		Completeness			Data Reliability	Failure Tolerance		Effectiveness		
Confidentiality					Data Timeliness	Flexibility/Robustness		Efficiency of Use		
Integrity					Data Validity	Reliability				
Safety						Scalability				
Non-Repudiation						Maintainability*				

Fig. 2. Trustworthiness attributes.

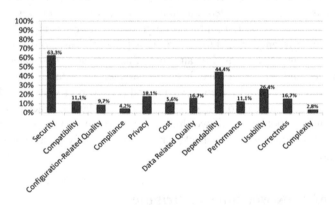

Fig. 3. Distribution of the SOTA in classified quality categories of trustworthiness attributes.

The definition of the trustworthiness attributes and their classified quality category is given in sub-sections bellow. Results of 72 relevant papers are presented in Fig. 3 as the distribution of the studies in different quality categories. A paper can obviously belong to multiple categories.

4.1 Security

Security covers the capability of a software system to protect entities against attacks and misuse despite certain vulnerabilities and to protect the access to resources. The sub-attributes of the security quality category are the following:

- **Accountability:** The state of being accountable, liable to be called on to render an account, the obligation to bear the consequences for failure to perform as expected.
- **Auditability/Traceability:** Capability of the service to be monitored and to generate in a reliable and secure way events producing an audit trail. Based on this audit a sequence of events can be reconstructed and examined. Security events could include authentication events, policy enforcement decisions, and others. The resulting audit trail may be used to detect attacks, confirm compliance with policy, deter abuse, or other purposes.
- **Confidentiality:** The ability to limit access to the system and its data only to authorised agents. It is defined as the absence of unauthorized disclosure of information.
- **Integrity:** The ability to ensure that the system and its data are not corrupted, improper system state alterations either accidental or malicious alternation or removal of information are prohibited.
- **Safety:** The ability to operate without risk of injury or harm to users and the system's environment. It can be achieved by absence of consequences on the users and the environment.
- **Non-Repudiation:** The ability to prove to the data sender that data have been delivered, and to prove the sender's identity to the recipient, so that neither the sender nor the recipient can deny operations of sending and receiving data.

4.2 Compatibility

Compatibility/Interoperability has been defined as the ability of diverse services to work constructively with each other. Actually, different services can coexist without side effects, without even knowing each other. Compatibility amounts to the necessity of two interacting parties to fulfil each other's constraints and, therefore, to correctly interact. The following sub-attributes belong to compatibility quality category:

- **Openness** means the system is designed in such a way that it is transparent how it works and how to connect to the system. This relates to other attributes like interoperability, transparency and extensibility [29, 30].
- **Reusability** can be defined on two levels, namely, syntactic level and operational. The former relies on type definition and type compatibility rules. The later is about operation signatures.

4.3 Configuration-Related Quality

This quality category contains quality attributes that influence the way a service is configured to function or characterize if the promised functional and quality level has been actually delivered during the service's lifetime period e.g., completeness, stability. The following sub-attributes belong to configuration-related quality category:

- **Change Cycle/Stability:** Change related to the service in terms of its interface and/ or implementation/recomposition.
- **Completeness:** A measure of the difference between the specified set of features (e.g., functions) and the implemented set of features.

4.4   Compliance

The service should comply with standards (e.g., industry specific standards) and/or regulations. This can affect a number of other attributes, such as e.g., the security, portability and interoperability of the service. Behaviour of a service should always comply with the user's expectation (specifications).

4.5   Privacy

In internet connected systems, privacy from a system perspective is viewed as the system's ability and functionality that allows users to take control of the usage of their private information. From this system perspective privacy is a strong contributor to trustworthiness of the system. Consequently, when designing systems the designers must ensure through their design process that the way in which the system will handle private information is in compliance with the local and international laws in order to render these systems as trustworthy.

4.6   Cost

Cost is a (composite) quality attribute consisting of three (atomic) service attributes: cost model, fixed costs and variable costs. Actually, cost can be computed either from all atomic cost attributes or only from the fixed costs attribute.

4.7   Data Related Quality

Data related quality (information and data quality) characterize input/output data by quality attributes that traditionally have been used in the information and data quality domains, e.g., accuracy and timeliness. The following sub-attributes belong to data related quality category:

- **Data Integrity:** It can be compromised by human errors, malicious attacks, intentional data modification, transmission errors, system/software bugs or viruses, or hardware malfunctions.
- **Data Reliability:** Correctness of the data used by the system. It depends on the sub-systems used as well as on the provenance of the data.
- **Data Timeliness:** The property of information being able to arrive early or at the right time.

- **Data Validity:** The data values satisfy acceptance requirements of the validation criteria or fall within the respective domain of acceptable values. Validity criteria are often based on "expert opinion" and are generally viewed as "rules of thumb" although some validity criteria may be based on established theory or scientific fact.

4.8 Dependability

Dependability of a computing system is the property/ability that reliance can justifiably be placed on the service it delivers. It also has been defined as a correct and predictable execution and ensured that, when executed, it functions as intended. In [14], dependability and trustworthiness are considered to have same goals while both suffering the same threats (faults, errors, and failures). The attributes belong to this quality category are as below:

- **Accuracy:** Definition of the error rate produced by the service calculated on the basis of the expected results.
- **Availability:** The ability to deliver services whenever it is required.
- **Failure Tolerance:** The ability of a service to provide its functionality to clients in case of failures. In general, it is the capability of a service to handle failures. The circumstances of service failures and how a service will react to failures are described. Compensation is its sub-attribute. It is the ability to undo the effects of a service invocation when using stateful services.
- **Flexibility/Robustness:** It refers to the capability of the service to behave in an acceptable way in anomalous or unexpected situations or when the context changes. Adaptability, reparability, self-healability, recoverability, predictability and survivability are grouped under this attribute.
- **Reliability:** The ability of a service to perform its required functions under stated conditions for a specified period of time (failure-free operation capability in specified circumstances and for a specified period of time).
- **Scalability:** The capability of increasing the computing capacity of the SP's computer system and the ability of the system to process more operations or transactions in a given period.
- **Maintainability** is the ability of a system to undergo evolution with the corollary that the system should be designed so that evolution is not likely to introduce new faults into the system [31]. Maintainability has been defined as the process of making engineering changes to the system by involving the system designers and installers. Therefore, it is in contrast to adaptability, which is the process of changing a system to configure it for its environment of use.

4.9 Performance

This quality category contains quality attributes that characterize how well a service performs. The following attributes belong to performance quality category:

- **Transaction Time:** Time elapsed while a service is processing a transaction.
- **Throughput:** It refers to the number of event responses handled during an interval. It can be further distinguished into input-data-throughput (arrival rate of user data in

the input channel), communication throughput (user data output to a channel) and processing throughput (amount of data processed).

- **Response Time:** The time that passes while the service is completing one complete transaction. Latency as sub-attribute of response time is the time passed from the arrival of the service request until the end of its execution/service. Latency itself has been constructed with Execution time and delay time in queue. The former is the time taken by a service to process its sequence of activities. The latter is the time it takes for a service request to actually be executed.

4.10   Usability

Usability/Representation collects all those quality attributes that can be measured subjectively according to user feedback. It refers to the ease with which a user can learn to operate, prepare input for, and interpret the output of the service. The attributes belong to usability quality category are described below:

- **Satisfaction:** Freedom from discomfort and positive attitudes towards the use of the service. Attractiveness as a sub-attribute is the capability of the service to attract the user and their trust (e.g., having contact information and pictures of staff).
- **Learnability:** Capability of the service to enable the user to learn how to apply/use it. Comprehensibility (sub-attribute) is the capability of the service to enable the user to understand whether its functionality is suitable, and how it can be used for particular tasks and under particular conditions of use. Perceivable content (sub-attribute) makes the service useable and understandable to users, unambiguous or difficult.
- **Effectiveness:** Accuracy and completeness with which users achieve specified goals.
- **Efficiency of Use:** Resources expended in relation to the accuracy and completeness with which users achieve their goals.

4.11   Correctness

Correctness deals with the system behaviour conformed to the formal specification (accordance to expected behaviour and the absence of improper system states).

4.12   Complexity

Complexity deals with highly fragmented composite services which in most cases would be considered less trustworthy than a more atomic one.

- **Composability** has been defined as the ability to create systems and applications with predictably satisfactory behaviour from components, subsystems, and other systems.

4.13   Further Trustworthiness Attributes: A Discussion

In the previous sub-sections we have analysed the trustworthiness attributes found in the literature. In this sub-section we complement the presented collection of trustworthiness attributes with the further attributes from realistic use-cases. We discuss two domains, context and application dependence of trustworthiness by looking at the realistic use-cases as following:

- **Ambient Assisted Living:** These systems are in health care domain and application. The set of attributes which have primarily been considered consists of availability, confidentiality, integrity, maintainability, reliability and safety, but also performance and timeliness.
- **Cyber Crisis Management:** These systems deal with critical infrastructures, thus, the major trustworthiness attributes to be considered are integrity, timeliness, correctness, failure tolerance, and availability.

Below are the attributes, which potentially contribute to trustworthiness but have not been addressed in literature:

- **Provability:** The service performs provably as expected, resp. as defined. This is more a property of the engineering process rather than of the service delivered, but should be taken into account as well.
- **Predictability:** In general, the service performs in such a way that the user can predict its behaviour, either according to past experience (=best practices), or just due to logic inference of activities.
- **Flexible Continuity:** In case the service does not perform as expected, or fails, then there is a process to not only fix the issue in adequate time, but also to inform the user, give them the chance to be involved, and to re-use the service as soon as possible. This relates to recoverability and flexibility, but specifically applies to situations with failure potential.
- **Level of Service** is defined as the type of QoS commitment given to the application or user. It is often part of contractual agreements and therefore is often expressed in measurable terms. Although less well treated in literature related to trustworthiness, it constitutes an important trustworthiness component in most business applications. This attribute should be part of the "performance" group of attributes.
- **Accessibility** defines whether the service is capable of serving requests, specifically to clients with limited capabilities. While many services are ready to use, they might not be accessible to specific clients. For instance, the connection between the service and the client is problematic or the service requests the clients to be able to read. This attribute should be part of the "usability" group of attributes.
- **Content Accessibility** is ensuring that the content of the service can be navigated and read by everyone, regardless of location, experience, or the type of computer technology used. It is also part of the "usability" group of attributes.
- **Data Accuracy** is defined as correctness of a data value or set of values as source in view of an expected level of exact computing. It should be part of the "data related qualities" set of attributes.

- **Data Completeness** is defined as the availability of all required data. Completeness can refer to both the temporal and spatial aspect of data quality.
- **Data Consistency** means that when a service fails and then restarts, or is evoked to different points in time, the data returned by the service should be still valid, respectively responding with the same result.
- **Resolution** denotes the granularity of information treated, and although being of good value for decision making, it does not reflect an attribute of the system in general.
- **Operability** is the capability of the service to enable the user to operate on it.

5 Deriving Metrics for Identified Trustworthiness Attributes

Identifying the components of trustworthiness and aiming to build them into software does not necessarily ensure the trustworthiness of the designed system. Therefore, there is a need for trustworthiness evaluation, i.e., measure and make the trustworthiness of the system evident [32]. As mentioned above, trustworthiness can be interpreted differently by users and organizations. Hence, trustworthiness may be evaluated with respect to different targets like: the confidentiality of sensitive information, the integrity of valuable information, the availability of critical data, the response time or the accuracy of outputs. This makes the evaluation of trustworthiness challenging.

We defined trustworthiness attribute as a property of the system that indicates its ability to prevent potential threats from becoming active, i.e., a resilience assurance that it will not produce an unacceptable outcome. Therefore, a trustworthiness attribute is defined as a characteristic of a system that encourages or discourages trust in the system, e.g., availability, reliability. Based on the state-of-the-art analysis, trustworthiness attributes (around 40) are identified that can potentially contribute to the trustworthiness of the system. This collection of attributes can be used as indicators of the overall trustworthiness. Trustworthiness attributes influence different phases of the software life-cycle. For instance, some attributes can be measured only at software execution time, while others belong specifically to the development process. There is a need for the systematic treatment of trustworthiness metrics throughout the entire software life-cycle.

The system design processes will benefit from trustworthiness evaluation. As observed above, by identifying which software characteristics measurably contribute to trustworthiness. Related literature mostly studies trustworthiness from a security perspective while assuming that single properties (certification, certain technologies or methodologies) of services lead to trustworthiness. Compared to this, such a one-dimensional approach is insufficient to capture all the factors that contribute to a system's trustworthiness. Instead, a multitude of attributes need to be taken into account. Multifaceted views and concepts of trustworthiness bring complexity in evaluation of trustworthiness.

Since each stakeholder can have different ideas on trustworthiness, a structured and acknowledged model for describing trustworthiness attributes is needed. This model ideally should include a set of acknowledged methods, mechanisms and means for measuring the previously defined trustworthiness attributes. Hereto, their evaluation can produce tangible results of the trustworthiness characteristics of software.

This section focuses on measures or metrics for identified trustworthiness attributes of the to-be-developed software, service or application. A set of attributes describes generic trustworthiness requirements. Each of these generic trustworthiness requirements need to be detailed during the requirements engineering activities to specify the exact level and expected quality of the attribute. One way of detailing such a requirement engineering step is to define a measure for each trustworthiness attribute for the software in question. The attributes can be further complemented with properties to allow a more fine-grained goal definition. We use the term metric as a standard for measuring attributes. It is a function that takes one or more property values and produces a measure related to an attribute, e.g., reliability of a system, overall trustworthiness of a system, average response time. Trustworthiness attributes presented in Sect. 4 describes generic non-functional requirements for any software to fulfill certain trustworthiness expectations. The development of metrics for different attributes leads to various levels of complexity. In some cases like integrity a common (universal) set of metrics that apply to any software is impossible. Therefore, it is necessary to define a process for the identification of metrics in the requirements engineering phase.

There are a number of different methods available for systematically defining metrics, among others [32]: Goal-Question-Metric (GQM), artificial intelligence assessment techniques, assembling and mapping practical, concrete, "bottom-up" measurement methods, intrinsically measurable components and formal modelling techniques. In this paper, we employ GQM in deriving metrics for trustworthiness attributes, because of its universality and simplicity. Furthermore, this approach is widely adopted in software engineering field.

5.1   The GQM Method

GQM is a generic way of developing metrics. It has been introduced by Basili and Rombach [32]. For each Goal (e.g., the different trustworthiness attributes), a set of questions is identified that helps in identifying what supports achieving the goal and subsequently metrics that measure the gradual fulfillment of the goal (or sub-goals thereof). GQM follows to main processes: (1) definition process as a top down approach (left hand side of Fig. 4) and (2) analysis process as a bottom-up approach (right hand side of Fig. 4). It handles the problem of how to decide, and what to measure to reach your goals by defining measurable goals [33, 34].

An important success factor for the metrics to be helpful in due course of the development process (independently of using agile or more traditional process models) is that the metric must be able to be applied during the development process itself, at different stages of the software development (potentially, using slight variants of the same metric). Yet it seems very unlikely that requirements engineers will develop individual metrics for each trustworthiness attribute. Consequently, it is our aim to simplify this process by preparing a set of questions with corresponding potential metrics that only need to be specified in more detail. We aim at providing plug-ins for existing requirements engineering tools. Table 1 shows the derived metrics for the integrity attribute from the security category as an example.

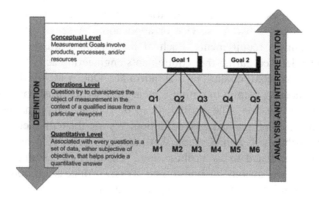

Fig. 4. The GQM Paradigm as a hierarchical structure [35].

Table 1. Example of GQM application for integrity metrics from security category.

Goal	Questions	Metric	Computation	Description
The data that is considered confidential used must be kept confidential at any time and at any place.	What percentage of interfaces needs authentication?	required authentication: % of interfaces which require authentication	x = (interfaces which require authentication / all interfaces) * 100%	This metric measure the interfaces which require authentication.
	Does the authorization follow the least privilege principle?	Least privilege's: % of authorization (objects) that are only used for authorizing one function/class etc.	x= number of authorization (objects) that are only used for authorizing one function/class etc./ number of authorization (objects) * 100%	This metric aims to reflect how granular the authorization required for executing a function, a class, etc. is (design principle: least privilege).

6   Conclusion and Future Work

STS lie at the intersection of the social aspects of people, society and organizations with the technical aspects and IS used by and underlying such social structures. A premise of the STS theory is that optimization of the socio-elements or the technical-elements of a system independently of each other will increase the unpredictable relationships inside the system, particularly the relationships that may be harmful to the system.

Trust can be viewed as a mechanism to reduce complexity in society and trustworthiness can be viewed as a driver for building trusting relationships. Hence, determining the system attributes that foster trustworthiness contributes to building and optimizing STS such that higher trust can be achieved in such systems.

To identify the attributes that foster trustworthiness we explored an extensive literature survey guided by earlier work in the S-Cube project [23] to identify software attributes related to trustworthiness. While passing through this survey, we also identified some software attributes that either have ambiguous definitions or their relationships to trust have not been well studied. The paper highlights several interesting issues about the subject of trustworthiness with respect to STS:

- The concept of trustworthiness needs rigorous specification and definition in the context of STS before we are able to build grounded trustworthiness measures.
- To be able to work operationally with trustworthiness attributes, metrics are necessary to set targets, measure progress, and identify the best possible investment by using ROI calculations. While this paper identifies software attributes that foster trustworthiness, it falls short of identifying software trustworthiness metrics that could be universally applied. Such metrics require further analysis and study.
- Trustworthiness in the context of STS includes some subjective component, and always will to some extent. To limit the subjective nature of any trustworthiness metric, a restriction of the context in which the metric is used will be essential.

Our future research will focus on some important questions:

- It is important to understand how the attributes identified in this paper actually influence trust by the users of the system. Empirical research is necessary, and needs to be carried out. Just as for the identification of the attributes, existing literature will only look at individual aspects.
- We need to understand how to identify interdependencies between different attributes, and how consequently to define a "profile" (=set of trustworthiness attributes) for a certain application area.
- Substantial work is needed to investigate existing development methodologies, and to show how they can be enhanced to enable taking trustworthiness attributes into account, in a measurable and comparable way.
- Current certification and attestation programs need to be investigated how they could benefit from taking a wider range of attributes into account than just those related to security, as it is mostly the case today.
- In view of this last research target, metrics shall be developed that express a quantitative view on the assurance of trustworthiness attributes respected/covered by the development practices.

Acknowledgements. The research leading to these results has received funding from the European Union's 7th Framework Programme FP7/2007-2013 under grant agreement 317631 (OPTET).

References

1. Pazos-Revilla, M., Siraj, A.: Tools and techniques for SSE-CMM implementation. In: 12th World Multi-Conference on Systemics, Cybernetics and Informatics, (2008)
2. Huang, L., Bai, X., Nair, S.: Developing a SSE-CMM-based security risk assessment process for patient-centered healthcare systems. In: 6th International Workshop on Software Quality, pp. 11–16. ACM, New York (2008)
3. Capability Maturity Model® Integration, Software Engineering Institute, Carnegie Mellon University Version 1.1

4. Sztompka, P.: Trust: A Sociological Theory. Cambridge University Press, Cambridge (1999)
5. Dahrendorf, R.: Reflections on the Revolution in Europe. Transaction Publishers, New Brunswick (2005)
6. Golembiewski, R., McConkie, M.: The centrality of interpersonal trust in group processes. In: Cooper, C.L. (ed.) Theories of Group Processes, pp. 131–185. Wiley, London (1975)
7. Deutsch, M.: Cooperation and trust: some theoretical notes. In: Jones, M.R. (ed.) Nebraska Symposium on Motivation, pp. 275–319. University of Nebraska Press, Lincoln (1962)
8. Shapiro, S.P.: The social control of impersonal trust. The Am. J. Sociol. **93**(3), 623–658 (1987)
9. Luhmann, N.: Trust and Power. Wiley, Chichester (1979)
10. Mei, H., Huang, G., Xie, T.: Internetware: a software paradigm for internet computing. Computer **45**(6), 26–31 (2012)
11. Sommerville, I.: Software Engineering. Perarson, London (2011)
12. OPTET Consortium: Project 317631 OPerational Trustworthiness Enabling Technologies, Annex I – Description of Work, Technical report, (2012)
13. Whitworth, B.: A Brief Introduction to Sociotechnical Systems. In: Khosrow-Pour, M. (ed.) Encyclopedia of Information Science and Technology, 2nd edn, pp. 394–400. IGI Global, CITY (2009)
14. Avizienis, A., Laprie, J.C., Randell, B., Landwehr, C.: Basic concepts and taxonomy of dependable and secure computing. IEEE Trans. Dependable Secure Comput. **1**(1), 11–33 (2004)
15. Li, M., Li, J., Song, H., Wu, D.: Risk management in the trustworthy software process: a novel risk and trustworthiness measurement model framework. In: 5th International Joint Conference on INC, IMS and IDC, pp. 214–219. IEEE Computer Society Press, Los Alamitos (2009)
16. ISO 15408-1, Common Criteria, 2009. Information technology – Security techniques – Evaluation criteria for IT security. Geneva, Switzerland
17. San-Martín, S., Camarero, C.: A cross-national study on online consumer perceptions, trust, and loyalty. J. Organ. Comput. Electron. Commer. **22**, 64–86 (2012)
18. Chen, C., Wang, K., Liao, S., Zhang, Q., Dai, Y.: A Novel server-based application execution architecture. In: International Conference on Computational Science and Engineering, 12th IEEE International Conference on Computational Science and Engineering, pp. 678–683, IEEE Computer Society Press, Los Alamitos (2009)
19. Harris, L.C., Goode, M.M.: The four levels of loyalty and the pivotal role of trust: a study of online service dynamics. J. Retail. **80**, 139–158 (2004)
20. Gómez, M., Carbó, J., Benac-Earle, C.: An anticipatory trust model for open distributed systems. In: Butz, M.V., Sigaud, O., Pezzulo, G., Baldassarre, G. (eds.) ABiALS 2006. LNCS (LNAI), vol. 4520, pp. 307–324. Springer, Heidelberg (2007)
21. Yolum, P., Singh, M.P.: Engineering self-organizing referral networks for trustworthy service selection. IEEE Trans. Syst. Man Cybern. Part A Syst. Hum. **35**(3), 396–407 (2005)
22. Yan, Z., Goel, G.: An adaptive trust control model for a trustworthy component software platform. In: Xiao, B., Yang, L.T., Ma, J., Muller-Schloer, C., Hua, Yu. (eds.) ATC 2007. LNCS, vol. 4610, pp. 226–238. Springer, Heidelberg (2007)
23. S-Cube: Quality Reference Model for SBA. Technical report, S-Cube European Network of Excellence (2008)
24. Boehm, B.W., Brown, J.R., Lipow, M.: Quantitative evaluation of software quality. In: 2nd International Conference on Software Engineering, pp. 592–605. IEEE Computer Society Press, Los Alamitos (1976)
25. Adrion, W.R., Branstad, M.A., Cherniavsky, J.C.: Validation, verification, and testing of computer software. ACM J. Comput. Surv. **14**(2), 159–192 (1982)

26. McCall, J.A., Richards, P.K., Walters, G.F.: Factors in Software Quality: US Department of Commerce, National Technical Information Service (1977)
27. ISO/IEC: ISO 9126-1: 2001, Software Engineering – Product quality – Part 1: Quality Model. Standard, International Organization of Standardization (2001)
28. Gol Mohammadi, N., Paulus, S., Bishr, M., Metzger, A., Koennecke, H., Hartenstein, S., Pohl, K.: An analysis of software quality attributes and their contribution to trustworthiness, In: 3rd International Conference on Cloud Computing and Services Science, Special Session on Security Governance and SLAs in Cloud Computing, (2013)
29. McKnight, D.H., Choudhury, V., Kacmar, C.: Developing and validating trust measures for e-Commerce: An integrative typology. J. Inf. Syst. Res. **13**(3), 334–359 (2002)
30. Patil, V., Shyamasundar, R.K.: Trust management for e-Transactions. Sadhana **30**(2–3), 141–158 (2005)
31. Sommerville, I., Dewsbury, G.: Dependable domestic systems design: a socio-technical approach. J. Interact. Comput. **19**(4), 438–456 (2007)
32. Paulus, S., Mohammadi, N.G., Weyer, T.: Trustworthy software development. In: De Decker, B., Dittmann, J., Kraetzer, C., Vielhauer, C. (eds.) CMS 2013. LNCS, vol. 8099, pp. 233–247. Springer, Heidelberg (2013)
33. Basili, V.R., Rombach, H.D.: The TAME Project: Towards improvement oriented software environments. IEEE Trans. Softw. Eng. **14**(6), 758–773 (1988)
34. Li, M., Li, J., Song, H., Wu, D.: Risk management in the trustworthy software process: a novel risk and trustworthiness measurement model framework. In: 5th International Joint Conference on INC, IMS and IDC, pp. 214–219. IEEE Computer Society Press, Los Alamitos (2009)
35. Herrmann, D.S.: Complete Guide to Security and Privacy Metrics: Measuring Regulatory Compliance, Operational Resilience, and ROI. Auerbach Publications, Boca Raton (2007)

Using Ontologies to Analyze Compliance Requirements of Cloud-Based Processes

Thorsten Humberg[2], Christian Wessel[1], Daniel Poggenpohl[2], Sven Wenzel[2(✉)],
Thomas Ruhroth[1], and Jan Jürjens[1,2]

[1] Chair of Software Engineering, Technical University Dortmund,
Dortmund, Germany
{christian.wessel,thomas.ruhroth}@cs.tu-dortmund.de
[2] Fraunhofer Institute for Software and Systems Engineering ISST,
Dortmund, Germany
{thorsten.humberg,daniel.poggenpohl,sven.wenzel}@isst.fraunhofer.de
http://jan.jurjens.de

Abstract. In recent years, the concept of cloud computing has seen a significant growth. The spectrum of available services covers most, if not all, aspects needed in existing business processes, allowing companies to outsource large parts of their IT infrastructure to cloud service providers. While this prospect might offer considerable economic advantages, it is hindered by concerns regarding information security as well as compliance issues. Relevant regulations are imposed by several sources, like legal regulations or standards for information security, amounting to an extend that makes it difficult to identify those aspects relevant for a given company. In order to support the identification of relevant regulations, we developed an approach to represent regulations in the form of ontologies, which can then be used to examine a given system for compliance requirements. Additional tool support is offered to check system models for certain properties that have been found relevant.

Keywords: Cloud computing · Compliance · Business processes · Risks · Ontologies

1 Introduction

Cloud computing enables reduction of costs and gains flexibility by outsourcing hard- and software, but running business processes in such environments poses new issues with respect to compliance and security compared to locally hosted solutions. Legal regulations such as data protection laws or the European directive Solvency II cause additional requirements to business processes and underlying software systems. Hence, before outsourcing a process or parts of it into the cloud, the processes and systems have to be checked with respect to these requirements.

In order to support compliant and secure outsourcing of business processes into cloud environments, we developed a two-step approach based on ontologies.

© Springer International Publishing Switzerland 2014
M. Helfert et al. (Eds.): CLOSER 2013, CCIS 453, pp. 36–51, 2014.
DOI: 10.1007/978-3-319-11561-0_3

The concept of ontologies is used to formalize various standards that contain regulations regarding IT-security as well as compliance aspects. We show how this can be applied to capture the content of these sources in a unified way, and detect dependencies and references between different source documents. Using this basic regulatory ontology, we enhance it with further semantic information concerning the actual aspects dealt with in particular parts of the regulatory documents.

When using this collection of information in an actual analysis of a system or process model, it is possible to identify specific situations that require further analysis to test if the constraints they impose on a process are met in the model. The constraints can be used to suggest corresponding examination methods from a repository of possible (automated) compliance or security checks.

The approach is supported by different analysis tools we developed. They are integrated into the model-based environment CARiSMA.

In the following section, we give an overview about the background concepts relevant to our approach. Section 3 presents the internal structure of our ontology as well as to how it can be created based on diverging sources of input. After formalizing the information, it can be used to investigate given models for situations to be considered (see Sect. 4). Section 5 presents various tools that have been integrated in the model analysis tool CARiSMA to support our analysis process. In Sect. 6 we present our ongoing work on the methodology. Related work is presented in Sect. 7, followed by a discussion of our approach as well as possible future developments in Sect. 8.

2   Background

This section introduces some terms before we explain our approach of ontology-based compliance formalization and analysis of business processes in the next section.

2.1   Cloud Computing

Cloud computing is generally regarded to be one of the major developments in information technology in recent years. Substituting existing self-maintained hard- and software with resources rented on an on-demand basis offers significant potential benefits, in particular a possible reduction of costs as well as a gain in flexibility. Especially for small and medium-sized businesses (SMB) it might be an appealing alternative to maintaining their own data centers. The American *National Institute of Standards and Technology* (NIST) subdivides Cloud Computing into three service levels. *Infrastructure as a Service (IaaS)*, is the lowest layer providing basic virtual hardware resources. This may include virtual machines or networks. *Platform as a Service (PaaS)*, represents a middleware for writing distributed and scalable software, which resides upon the IaaS layer. *Software as a Service (SaaS)* is the top-most layer with ready-to-use software which was built using PaaS solutions.

Depending on the chosen layer type, different security needs have to be considered. If an IaaS structure was chosen, only the bare virtual hardware is provided. All security needs have to be installed and checked starting from the operating system and ending with the software that is executed on it. All security requirements are in the hands of the customer of the cloud service. With PaaS it is necessary that the software developed on top of it meets the security standards needed for the business process. On the SaaS layer software must be chosen, that complies with the security needs and meets the compliance requirements.

The required security level further depends on other characteristics like the deployment model, e.g., private cloud versus public clouds. While private clouds can be considered relatively secure against attacks from outside they are exposed to internal attackers. Public clouds on the other hand need to be protected against attacks from the outside.

2.2   Risk and Compliance

In this paper we speak of risks meaning the components mentioned in the *IT-Grundschutz Catalogues* [1]. We do neither consider probability of occurrence nor amount of damage caused by them. Risks in our understanding are IT security related while compliance is seen as laws or internal regulations which have to be held. There exists a tight bounding between security risk, security and compliance as for example compliance rules are not met when an attacker is able to retrieve personal data from a not properly secured server.

Risks. In this context a risk is defined as an IT security related vulnerability in a business process which is executed in a cloud environment. Examples are unsecured communication channels between cloud hosts, insufficient rights management or processing of confidential data.

Compliance. A security analysis of the cloud computing environment should be carried out before a security requirement analysis is performed on the business operation. This will yield the maximum number of security requirements that can be met.

The conformance to compliance regulations should be audited on three levels.

Process and Compliance Analysis. Documents from which business processes can be derived should be analyzed. Our approach considers processes given in form of process models (e.g. UML activity diagrams or BPMN models). The risk analysis also works on less structured documents such as textual process descriptions or log files from which processes can be mined.

Design Time Compliance. The implementation of a business process has to comply with legal regulations and company policies. The cloud interface, the activities performed within the cloud, and the data flows between cloud and user are the major points of interest. Furthermore, the overall consistency of the processes with respect to compliance requirements should be verified.

Runtime Compliance. It has to be ensured that all compliance-relevant and critical processes (esp. those outsourced into a cloud) are monitored and logged.

Such a monitoring can be performed using business process mining and conformance checking [2]. Our approach enables the identification of such processes. The runtime analysis itself is not further considered in this paper.

2.3   Ontologies

Ontologies are a widely used tool to describe incomplete information about an area. In contrast to models having a closed world assumption, ontologies employ an open world assumption, i.e. they can be extended arbitrarily. In this paper we use the *Web Ontology Language* (OWL) [3]. OWL knows three profiles which differ in expressiveness and the possibility to reason about facts in the ontology. The least expressive profile is OWL-Lite. The OWL profile OWL-DL is semantically equivalent to the Description Logic [4]. And OWL-FULL allows on one hand the largest expressiveness but is on the other hand not always decidable.

In this paper we use OWL-FULL for the sake of simplicity. It allows us to use smaller ontologies in our context.

A graphical representation of an ontology is depicted in Fig. 1: The basic elements of ontologies are the classes (also called concepts, depicted as rectangles, e.g., **Rule**) and the individuals (ovals, e.g. *Plan_Investment*). Classes can be seen as a set of individuals sharing common properties. The membership of an individual to a class is depicted using a dashed line with a triangle arrow. Thus *Approve_Investment* is an individual in the class **Activity**. The concepts can be related by an is-a relation (solid line with triangle arrow, e.g. **MARiskRule** is-a **Rule**), describing that all individuals of a class also belong to the superclass. Classes can be defined directly or by operations like the intersection of classes.

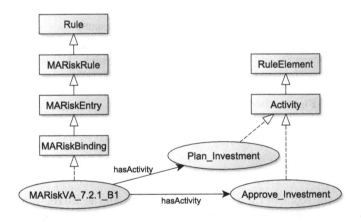

Fig. 1. Part of the ontology's class structure: **Rule**, **RuleElement**, and subclasses.

Relationships between different individuals are expressed with roles. Roles are used as a directed property, hence, we use an arrow as a graphical representation (see. Fig. 1) together with a descriptive name.

3   Regulatory Ontology

The principle of ontologies is especially suited for formalizing compliance regulations. With the classification provided by distinct concepts, information can be represented in a structured way, allowing for its utilization in automated analysis methods. At the same time, it is still possible to capture the diverse structures found in different types of relevant input standards. Furthermore, it is possible to express relations between entities across different inputs.

An outline of our ontology used to store the compliance information is given in Fig. 2. All classes to be used are derived from one of the depicted groups.

Rule. Individuals of this class and its subconcepts are used to store the information directly imported from the source documents.

RuleElements. contain semantical enhancements, describing different aspects a rule can refer to, e.g. referred activities and roles.

Situation. represents a more complex setting given by a rule, e.g. the referenced concept of Separation of Duty.

Constraint. indicates how a specific situation can be (automatically) checked in a given model.

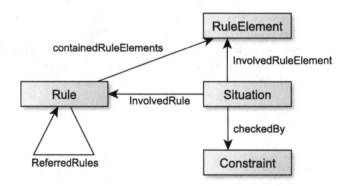

Fig. 2. Main concepts of the regulatory ontology.

In the following sections, these classes are explained in more detail.

3.1   Rules

Depending on the scope of the analysis, different standards are relevant. Some are focused on IT-security, e.g. the ISO 27k series [5] or the IT-Grundschutz Catalogues [1] published by the German Federal Office for Information Security (BSI). Particularly important in the field of cloud computing are regulations concerning compliance issues. Examples include national laws regarding data privacy and regulations relevant to specific sectors, e.g. Solvency II for financial institutions.

Regulations are generally given in the form of textual descriptions, with differing internal structures, thus being inconvenient for automated processing.

To overcome these restrictions, it is necessary to represent their content in a unified way.

The ontology's concept of classes with inheritance offers a method to capture those structures in a way that on the one hand preserves this information, but on the other hand still provides enough uniformity to use automated analysis methods.

Two types of classes are used at this stage: Those that contain the actual content, and others that represent the *structure* the content is organised in. Both classes are derived from **Rule**, but only the classes forming the content are evaluated in our automated processing.

Additionally, object properties are used to capture references between rules. These references may exist between rules within the same standard as well as between different input sources.

An example is shown in Fig. 1: The left hand side shows how the concept **MARiskBinding** is derived from **Rule** via several steps, and instantiated by the individual *MARiskVA_7.2.1_B1*, representing a specific entry from the document.

Creating the basic individuals representing the content of a standard is mainly a transformation. The generation of this stage can in general be fully automated, depending on the format the input is available in. For example, the catalogues provided by the BSI are available in HTML format and allow for an automatic conversion into the ontology.

3.2   Rule Elements

Based on the mere representation of the content, the ontology can be enriched with further details, namely *Rule Elements*.

An individual of the concept **RuleElement** (or subconcept thereof) can constitute any aspect relevant for a rule contained in the ontology.

Currently we define five types of elements. New concepts can easily be added as required.

Artifact. Representing objects a standard refers to, e.g. documents or IT hardware

Role. Specific roles mentioned, e.g. executives or data protection officer

Activity. Certain action, i.e. from a business process model, e.g. reporting required information

Process. A more complex operation, potentially involving several activities

Property. Requirements demanded by a standard, e.g. confidentiality or non-repudiation

The usage of rule elements directly yields the possible application of related properties: There are property relations from individuals of class **Rule** (or subclasses thereof) to those individuals representing rule elements that are relevant for the particular rule.

Object properties between instances of rule elements can be added to the ontology, but are currently not evaluated in our approach.

In contrast to converting the text content, identification of rule elements requires the interpretation of the textual representation. Given this problem, it is not yet possible to fully automate this step. As a first foundation we defined a set of typical elements with associated keywords. Identifying those keywords, or synonyms thereof, can be used to generate occurrences of specific elements.

In order to fully utilize the advantages of the approach, a manual enhancement is still necessary. A specialized tool for this purpose is integrated into our environment and described in Sect. 5.

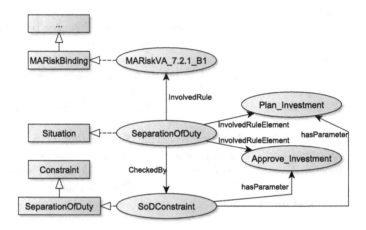

Fig. 3. Extract from the ontology, representing the Situation "Separation of Duties".

3.3   Situations and Constraints

Based on rule elements, we define *situations* as generic patterns that can occur in an examined model. Within the ontology, a situation links to a set of rule elements (via the *InvolvedRuleElement*-property). The presence of those elements in a model indicates the possible relevance of the particular situation. Additionally, an object property links to the particular rules the situation originates from.

A popular example is the need to implement the *separation of duty* pattern within a business process: In this case, a pair of activities must not be executed by the same person. The involved elements in this case are instances of the two activities. This is modeled in the ontology as shown in Fig. 3: *SeparationOfDuty* is an individual of the concept **Situation**, described in the **Rule** individual *MARiskVA_7.2.1_B1*. It forbids the activities *Plan_Investment* and *Approve_Investment* to be carried out by the same person. As shown in Fig. 1, both activities are instanciated from the RuleElement concept **Activity**.

To contain this specific situation, an actual business process model must thus contain two activities corresponding to *Plan_Investment* and *Approve_Investment*. Details on how those are identified are given in Sect. 4.

Though a situation does not in itself contain information about how it is to be tested on an actual model, it can reference to individuals of the class **Constraint**. If a process contains a situation, the corresponding constraints of the situation have to be respected for the process to be secure. The constraints can be further parameterized using rule elements. Only rule elements applicable to the situation, i.e. associated with the rules involved in it, can be used as parameters. Constraints can vary in their implementation, ranging from textual descriptions to automated checks available in the CARiSMA framework.

Formalizing possible situations and assigning appropriate constraints is a manual task as well. It consists of identifying the necessary components and creating a new individual for this situation.

The generation of this compliance ontology is a general preparation step for our process analysis. Regardless, it is only defined by the considered input standards.

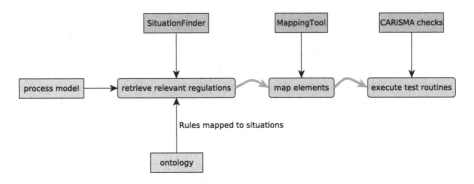

Fig. 4. Business process analysis overview.

4   Process Analysis

In the previous section we showed how the ontology used by the analysis process is designed and created to support the analysis of business processes. In this section we explain how compliance and regulatory requirements in business processes are identified and verified. The input for this process is a formal model of the business process in form of e.g. a BPMN model and the ontology containing the necessary regulations.

The analysis itself consists of three steps, namely:

1. Identification of relevant rule elements (i.e. situations in which this rule elements occur) within the regulations applicable to the business process that should be analyzed.
2. Mapping of the business process model elements to rule elements of the applicable situation.

3. Verification of the rule element constraints imposed by the situation. An example would be a check testing whether a *separation of duty* constraint on the business process is met.

Figure 4 gives a global view over the analysis process. The process is discussed in more detail in what follows.

Identification of Relevant Rules. For the first step in the analysis process it is necessary to identify situations (see Sect. 3.3) in the process model which have to be checked. As shown in the previous section a situation consists of one or more rules and part of the rule elements present in these rules, which may be involved persons (roles), objects or activities.

For example in the separation of duty constraint mentioned before, there are two actions involved: *"Plan_Investment"* and *"Approve_Investment"*. As these are individuals of the concept **Activity** they can be seen as keywords during a search for the situation "separation of duty (SoD)". The idea behind this is to test the names of the activities of the business process model for accordance with individuals of the ontology. In this step all labels of all model elements (e.g. text comments, labels on transitions, etc.) of the analyzed process are tested.

If all rule elements of a situation can be found among the labels of a business process model, the according checks for this situation will be suggested to the user. Since the search for an exact match between an activity name and a name of an individual may be ineffective, we utilize word databases which consider co-occurrent words and synonyms of an activity name. Thereby we utilize the following scoring system.

First we define a constant score s. If a word of a label is found directly as a keyword of a i-th rule element it will produce a score $s_i = s$. We define a score $s_i = \frac{s}{2}$ for matches found via synonyms of the word of the label because it is not the original word but at least semantically equivalent. Matches found with co-occurrent words have the lowest score of $s_i = \frac{s}{4}$ since the original word of the label is not involved any more. The final score S is then calculated with $S = \sum_{i=1}^{n} s_i$ where n is the number of rule elements which are involved in the specific situation. M is defined as the maximum reachable score, which is built using $n \times s$, where n is the above-mentioned number of rule elements the situation is built of. We avoid too many false-positive matches by discarding those below a certain threshold t. Therefore only matches which satisfy $M - S < t$ are considered for the subsequent analysis.

In order to get an almost complete set of applicable situations for a given business process model we expand the result by other potential situations which may be of interest to test. Usually regulations have cross references to other associated regulations. These can be found easily utilizing the ontology described in the previous section.

For example the SoD mentioned above is a *Situation* individual which has an involved rule (an object property) *MaRiskVA_7.2.1_B1* which is a **MARiskBinding** individual. *MaRiskVA_7.2.1_B1* may have object properties to instances of other rules. Situations associated to these rules are added to the result set and their corresponding checks are additionally recommended to the user.

Mapping of Elements. Every situation has one or more constraints that have to be met by the analyzed process model. Some of these constraints could be verified with the aid of specialized tools, e.g. CARiSMA. In order to realize tool-based checking of situations it is necessary to specify the parameters, i.e. to name the actors, the activities and objects used in a specific situation.

Therefore the second step in the analysis process is to map the elements of the business process model to parameters of the check. This is a manual task, because model elements can be named individually by the modeler of the process. For example the name of the *applicant* role in the separation of duty scenario may be an arbitrary value, which can not be determined automatically.

Constraint Checking. After all model elements have been mapped to rule elements the constraints for a specific situation can be verified. This can be accomplished in various ways. A constraint may be verified by an automated test routine that systematically analyzes a given formal model, e.g. a BPMN or UML model with regard to whether specific requirements for a model are met.

Automated verification may be implemented as a CARiSMA check. In this case, the mapping of constraints of the ontology to corresponding checks in CARiSMA is stored in a file separate from the ontology. Doing this, the ontology itself remains reusable and uncluttered by implementation-specific information.

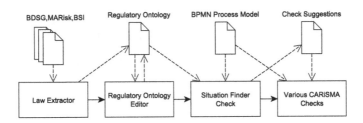

Fig. 5. Regulatory toolchain.

5   Tool Support

This section provides an overview of the various implementation efforts providing the tool support for creating and editing the regulatory ontology used during the analysis. The tools have been integrated with CARiSMA[1], our Eclipse-based environment for model analysis. First we describe the extractor used to create the ontology using various law documents. We then show the front end with which one is able to create the various other concepts and relations of the ontology. The enriched ontology can be used during process analysis to determine the

---
[1] http://carisma.umlsec.de

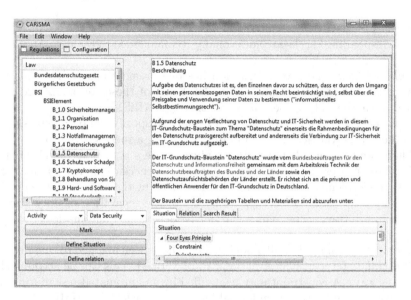

Fig. 6. Regulatory Ontology Editor.

checks to use during an analysis. The CARiSMA *Situation Finder Check* is one possible way to identify applicable situations. The process tool chain is visualized in Fig. 5.

Law Extractor. This tool parses regulatory documents of various formats to create the rule individuals of the regulatory ontology. Currently supported are the MARisk [6], the BDSG [7] and BGB [8], and the BSI catalogues [1]. The resulting OWL ontology can then be modified using the following tools.

Regulatory Ontology Editor. After extracting the rules, the ontology can then be enriched with the regulatory ontology editor depicted in Fig. 6. Text passages can be marked and stored as individuals of the rule element subconcepts. Situations can be created by selecting the rule elements that comprise the situation and naming it appropriately. Constraints that can be imposed on situations are parameterized with rule element subconcepts. Constraint individuals can then be assigned to situations, using the situational rule elements to set the parameters of the constraint.

In addition to the integrated GUI, we have implemented a web-based version provides the possibility for distributed access to the ontology.

Situation Finder Check. There are many possible solutions to determine which situations apply during the execution of a given process. As an exemplary implementation of the methods for situation identification the Situation Finder checks if a given BPMN process model contains all the rule elements that define a situation. If all are present in the process, the check then outputs the appropriate checks that should be run on the given model in order to verify its validity with regards to the regulations. Other methods for identifying situations could potentially involve references between rules or weighted approximations based on the types of rule elements in a situation.

Checks for Process Analysis. CARiSMA provides some checks that support the automated process analysis of models. For example, the check for the above-mentioned SoD constraint analyzes whether the conflicting actions are executed by different actors. In the case of a BPMN model this is achieved by checking the lanes the actions are embedded in. If the actions are in different lanes, the actors are different and the test passes. If the actions are in the same lane, the test fails and the check reports this to the user. Success or failure of the check is reported in two ways. On the one hand a textual report is generated and on the other hand the user is informed in a graphical manner by coloring of the failed actions directly in the diagram.

6 Support for Evolving Requirements

At the moment we are working on extending the approach for the use and adaption of referenced compliance documents. Many companies have internal guidelines which are built on top of existing guidelines like the BSI IT-Grundschutz Catalogues. So they can define which parts are implemented as well as the definition of new internal guidelines. Also the adaption and modification of the used guidelines is applied. Since each of these referenced or included documents can change interdependently we need a system to tackle the evolution and reaction of these evolutions.

To implement this needs, we use a technique under development in the SecVolution project [9,10] called *layered ontologies*. Layered ontologies are an extension of the OWL import function. The OWL import allows to import OWL ontologies and thus the extension of the imported ontologies. We extend this approach by adding *modification operators* such that parts of the imported ontologies can be hidden or changed:

The hide operation is used to remove parts of the imported ontologies and the change operator can change values in the ontology.

Sometimes the imported ontologies (resp. guidelines) are built using the layered ontologies approach itself. Here, we have a problem if parts of the ontologies can be hidden by a higher layer used by the current layer. Therefore, we include an unhide operation, which reverts the effect of a hide operation (see Fig. 7). Similar, we define a reset operation for undoing the change operation.

Compatibility with the described approach is maintained by expanding all ontology imports and modifications into a single flat separate ontology. Thus this approach can be easily integrated into the approach from the leading sections.

The layered ontologies approach also includes techniques to deal with evolution of imported guidelines. Whenever an imported ontology is changed, this modification can be analyzed and the using layers are semiautomatic co-evolved.

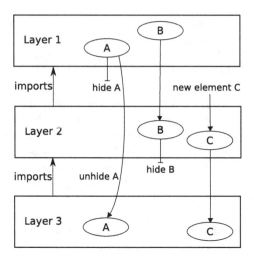

Fig. 7. Example depicting the hide and implicit add operation within three layers of ontologies.

User interaction is needed to provide decisions in ambiguous evolution cases as well as when new information like names are needed.

7   Related Work

The fulfillment of compliance and security requirements in business processes is essential to receive acceptance from customers. An approach to encode and check security requirements in BPMN models has been presented by Wolter et al. [11]. However, these requirements focus only on closed systems.

Cloud computing, which has lasted on the peak of Gartner's technology hype cycle [12] for quite a while now, leads to outsourcing of processes into heterogeneous environments. The use of cloud computing technologies offers economic potential for small and medium-sized enterprises. However, serious doubts wrt. security and compliance exist [13]. Hence, security approaches for closed systems are not eligible here. Menzel et al. [14] propose an approach to define security requirements on service orchestration level.

CloudCycle[2] is a project related to our approach. It focuses on cloud providers and offers services that allow them to guarantee their customers that they are compliant with security policies and further regulations. The approach of Cloud-Cycle   is   a   suitable   complement   for   our   approach.   Once   business processes are successfully outsourced into the cloud their security and compliance can be monitored.

Ontologies for cloud computing and cloud security have been presented by Gräuler et al. [15]. They analyzed the different sources of risks within cloud

---

[2] http://www.cloudcycle.org

computing environments and manifested them in an ontology. Based on that ontology, they provide a database of cloud providers that allows users to select a provider based on certain security properties. This is especially interesting for finding a suitable cloud provider after potential risks of a business process have been revealed by our approach.

Tsoumas and Gritzalis provide an ontology-based approach to organize security knowledge [16]. It is designed to enable reuse of knowledge and map requirements to implemented controls of a system. A similar approach to formalize security knowledge has been presented by Fenz and Ekelhart [17]. It focuses on representing security domain knowledge and corporate knowledge in an ontology. While we provide a systematic approach to represent the regulatory documents and to extract security or compliance requirements, the above-mentioned approaches consider only the modeling resulting security knowledge. It would be interesting to consider an integration of those approaches such that they could be used to represent the knowledge that is extracted by our approach.

Peschke et al. [18] present the *RiskFinder* which is a precursor of our risk analysis component. It analyses UML models with respect to security relevant vocabulary. Schneider et al. propose a heuristic search based on Bayesian filters [19]. HeRA realizes a feedback-driven approach for security analysis during requirements engineering [20]. These approaches provide powerful rules, however, they work only on single words and do not consider language databases.

Our view of IT security risks corresponds to the use in the BSI IT-Grundschutz Catalogues [1], which does not include concrete values for probabilities and possible extend of damage (or benefit) of risks. In the terminology defined by other standards, this information is included, e.g. in the ISO 27000 series [21] and NIST standard 800-39 [22].

8   Conclusions and Outlook

When outsourcing business processes into cloud environments, problems regarding security and compliance still represent major obstacles. The methodology described in this paper aims at supporting users in examining models of their systems and processes for potential risks. While a completely automated analysis still appears far from feasible, our approach and tools can aid in highlighting aspects that require further examination, either manually or tool-supported.

Using ontologies, one can take advantage of a very flexible, yet formalized, way of representing information, making it accessible for automated procedures.

Beside continuing our research regarding evolving requirements, several points seem worth considering to further develop our concept. Those include enhancement of tool-support, improvement of existing heuristics for the detection of matchings as well as support for established methods in knowledge systems, e.g. automated reasoning.

Acknowledgements. Parts of this research have been funded by the DFG project SecVolution (JU 2734/2-1 and SCHN 1072/4-1) which is part of the priority programme SPP 1593 "Design For Future - Managed Software Evolution".

Other parts have been funded by BMBF grants 01IS11008C and 01IS11008D (SecureClouds).

References

1. Bundesamt für Sicherheit in der Informationstechnik: BSI-Grundschutz Katalog (2006)
2. van der Aalst, W., Reijers, H., Weijters, A., Vandongen, B., Alvesdemedeiros, A., Song, M., Verbeek, H.: Business process mining: an industrial application. Inf. Syst. **32**(5), 713–732 (2007)
3. W3C OWL Working Group: OWL 2 Web Ontology Language: Document Overview (Second Edition). W3C Recommendation, 11 December 2012. http://www.w3.org/TR/owl2-overview/
4. Baader, F., Calvanese, D., McGuinness, D.L., Nardi, D., Patel-Schneider, P.F. (eds.): The Description Logic Handbook: Theory, Implementation, and Applications. Cambridge University Press, New York (2003)
5. ISO/IEC: ISO27001: Information Security Management System (ISMS) standard, October 2005. http://www.27000.org/iso-27001.htm
6. Bundesanstalt für Finanzdienstleistungsaufsicht: Mindestanforderungen an das Risikomanagement - MaRisk, October 2012
7. Bundesrepublik Deutschland, vertreten durch das Bundesministerium der Justiz.: Bundesdatenschutzgesetz, December 1990
8. Bundesrepublik Deutschland, vertreten durch das Bundesministerium der Justiz.: Bürgerliches Gesetzbuch, August 1896
9. SecVolution   Webpage: http://www-secse.cs.tu-dortmund.de/secse/pages/research/projects/SecVolution
10. Jürjens, J., Schneider, K.: Beyond one-shot security. In: Modelling and Quality in Requirements Engineering (Essays Dedicated to Martin Glinz on the Occasion of His 60th Birthday), Verlagshaus Monsenstein und Vannerdat, pp. 131–141 (2012)
11. Wolter, C., Menzel, M., Meinel, C.: Modelling security goals in business processes. In: Modellierung (2008)
12. Dixon, J., Jones, T.: Hype cycle for business process management. Technical report, Gartner Study (2011)
13. BITKOM: Cloud-Computing - Evolution in der Technik. Technical report, BITKOM (2009)
14. Menzel, M., Thomas, I., Meinel, C.: Security requirements specification in service-oriented business process management. In: ARES (2009)
15. Gräuler, M., Martens, B.; Teuteberg, F.: IT-Sicherheitsmanagement im Cloud Computing - Entwicklung und Implementierung einer Ontologie. In: Proceedings zur INFORMATIK 2011 (2011)
16. Tsoumas, B., Gritzalis, D.: Towards an ontology-based security management. In: Proceedings of the 20th International Conference on Advanced Information Networking and Applications (AINA), vol. 1, pp. 985–992. IEEE (2006)
17. Fenz, S., Ekelhart, A.: Formalizing information security knowledge. In: Proceedings of the 4th International Symposium on Information, Computer, and Communications Security (ASIACCS), p. 183. ACM Press, New York (2009)

18. Peschke, M., Hirsch, M., Jürjens, J., Braun, S.: Werkzeuggestützte Identifikation von IT-Sicherheitsrisiken. In: D-A-CH Security 2011 (2011)
19. Schneider, K., Knauss, E., Houmb, S., Islam, S., Jürjens, J.: Enhancing security requirements engineering by organizational learning. Requirements Eng., 1–22 (2011). doi:10.1007/s00766-011-0141-0
20. Knauss, E., Lubke, D., Meyer, S.: Feedback-driven requirements engineering: the heuristic requirements assistant. In: Proceedings of the 31st International Conference on Software Engineering, ICSE '09, pp. 587–590. IEEE Computer Society, Washington, DC (2009)
21. ISO/IEC: ISO27005: Information technology - Security techniques - Information security risk management, June 2008. http://www.27000.org/iso-27005.htm
22. NIST, Aroms, E.: NIST Special Publication 800–39 Managing Information Security Risk. CreateSpace, Paramount, CA (2012)

Assessing Latency in Cloud Gaming

Ulrich Lampe[1(✉)], Qiong Wu[1], Sheip Dargutev[1], Ronny Hans[1],
André Miede[2], and Ralf Steinmetz[1]

[1] Multimedia Communications Lab (KOM), TU Darmstadt,
Rundeturmstr. 10, 64283 Darmstadt, Germany
{ulrich.lampe,qiong.wu,sheip.dargutev,
ronny.hans,ralf.steinmetz}@KOM.tu-darmstadt.de
[2] Fakultät für Ingenieurwissenschaften, htw saar,
Goebenstr. 40, 66117 Saarbrücken, Germany
andre.miede@htwsaar.de

Abstract. With the emergence of cloud computing, diverse types of
Information Technology services are increasingly provisioned through
large data centers via the Internet. A relatively novel service category is
cloud gaming, where video games are executed in the cloud and delivered to a client as audio/video stream. While cloud gaming substantially reduces the demand of computational power on the client side, thus
enabling the use of thin clients, it may also affect the Quality of Service
through the introduction of network latencies. In this work, we quantitatively examined this effect, using a self-developed measurement tool and
a set of actual cloud gaming providers. For the two providers and three
games in our experiment, we found absolute increases in latency between
approximately 40 ms and 150 ms, or between 85 % and 800 % in relative
terms, compared to a local game execution. In addition, based on a second complementary experiment, we found mean round-trip times ranging
from about 30 ms to 380 ms using WLAN and approximately 40 ms to
1050 ms using UMTS between a local computer and globally distributed
compute nodes. Bilaterally among the compute nodes, results were in the
range from approximately 10 ms to 530 ms. This highlights the importance of data center placement for the provision of cloud gaming services
with adequate Quality of Service properties.

Keywords: Cloud computing · Cloud gaming · Quality of Service ·
Latency · Measurement

1 Introduction

Since its popularization in the mid-2000s, cloud computing has substantially
altered the way in which Information Technology (IT) services are delivered and
brought massive changes to the IT sector [1]. Today, the decade-old vision of
delivering IT as a "utility" has come closer to realization than ever before [2].
A relatively novel business model, within the greater context of cloud computing, is *cloud gaming*. The principal idea of this concept is to execute video games

© Springer International Publishing Switzerland 2014
M. Helfert et al. (Eds.): CLOSER 2013, CCIS 453, pp. 52–68, 2014.
DOI: 10.1007/978-3-319-11561-0_4

in a cloud data center and deliver them to a client as audio/video stream via the Internet. The client thus serves as a simple playback and input device; the computationally complex task of executing the actual game logic and rendering the game images is shifted to the cloud [3–6]. From a formal standpoint, based on the popular NIST definition of cloud computing [7], cloud gaming can most intuitively be interpreted as a subclass of the *Software as a Service* model, because it constitutes a functionally complex service that is offered on the basis of low-level infrastructure services.

From a customer perspective, one main advantage of cloud gaming exists in the ability to access games at any place and time, independent of any specific device upon which they are installed [3]. Furthermore, hardware expenditures are substantially reduced, because a simplistic thin client is usually sufficient for access [8]. In addition, games do not have to be purchased for a fixed (and commonly quite notable) amount of money, but can be leased on a pay-per-use basis. From the provider perspective, one main benefit is the prevention of copyright infringements [5]. Furthermore, the development process may be greatly simplified if games are exclusively developed for the cloud, rather than multiple different platforms.

However, the use of the Internet also introduces a new component into the delivery chain. Being a public network, the Internet lies (partially) out of the control sphere of both the user and the provider, and follows a "best effort" philosophy, i. e., it does not make any end-to-end Quality of Service (QoS) assurances [9]. Hence, limitations of the network infrastructure, such as high latency, small bandwidth, or high packet loss, may potentially affect the QoS of the *overall* cloud gaming system for the user.

In this work, we focus on the QoS parameter of latency. This parameter plays an important role for the overall game experience [6,10]. This specifically applies for action-oriented games such as first-person shooters, where it may determine whether a player is "fragged", i.e., her/his character is killed, or is able to frag her/his opponent [10,11]. Hence, the first research question we aim to empirically answer in this work is: "What is the impact of cloud gaming on the QoS parameter of latency, as compared to a local execution of a video game?". In addition, inspired by related research [3] and our own previous work [12], we formulate the following second research question: "What is the impact of the geographical placement of cloud data centers on the QoS parameter of latency?".

In the following Sect. 2, we address the first research question, concerning the difference between cloud-based and local gaming. This includes an extensive description of our procedure and a thorough presentation and discussion of results. The second research question, concerning the latency implications of global data center placement, is addressed in Sect. 3. An overview of related work is given in Sect. 4. The paper closes with a summary and general conclusions in Sect. 5.

2 Examination of Latency in Cloud-Based and Local Gaming

In this section, we describe the first part of our experiments, aiming at the quantification of latencies in cloud-based and local gaming. Following a description of the considered variables, the measurement tool, and the measurement procedure, we present our results and along with a thorough discussion.

2.1 Considered Variables

As explained in the previous section, in this work, we focus on the QoS parameter of latency. It thus constitutes the only *dependent* variable in our experiments. More specifically, we consider *user-perceived latency*. By that term, we refer to the timespan that elapses between a certain *action* performed by the user, e.g., the press of a mouse button or a key, and the corresponding game *reaction*, e.g., the appearance of gunfire or the menu. It is also referred to as "interactive response time" or "response delay" in related research [3,13]. Based on the combined findings of Choy et al., Wang, and Wilson latency can be split into the following components if a game is locally executed [3,14,15]:

- *Input lag*, which corresponds to the timespan between two subsequent sampling events of the game controller, e.g., mouse or keyboard.
- *Game pipeline CPU time*, i. e., the time which is required for processing the input and realizing the game logic.
- *Game pipeline GPU time*, i. e., the time which the graphic card requires for rendering the next frame of the game.
- *Frame transmission*, which denotes the time that is required for transferring the frame from the backbuffer to the frontbuffer of the graphic card, and subsequently to the screen.
- *LCD response time*, which indicates the timespan that is required to actually display the frame on the screen.

Once a game is executed in the cloud and delivered via a network, the following additional components have to be considered [3,14,15]:

- *Upstream data transfer*, i. e., the time that it takes to sent the user input to the cloud gaming provider.
- *Capture and encoding*, which denotes the time requirements for capturing the current frame and encoding it as video stream.
- *Downstream data transfer*, i. e., the timespan for transferring the stream to the client.
- *Decoding*, which indicates the time for converting the video stream back into a frame.

Intuitively, one might reason that a cloud-based game will always exhibit a higher latency that a locally executed game due to the additional latency components. However, this is not necessarily true. In fact, due to the use of potent hardware in the cloud and depending on the geographical distance between the user and the cloud provider, the reduction of time spent in the game pipeline may overcompensate the network, encoding, and decoding latencies [14].

The dependent variable in our experiment, latency, may potentially be determined by various factors, i. e., a set of *independent* variables. In our work, we focus on different games, cloud gaming providers, and network connections as suspected key determinants.

With respect to the main subject of our research, i. e., the examined games, our focus was on action-oriented titles. As briefly explained in Sect. 1, these games are commonly very sensitive to latency increases and thus, of elevated interest. We specifically chose the following titles, all of which are available both in the cloud and for local installation:

- *Shadowgrounds*[1] is a 3D first-person shooter game developed by Frozenbyte. It was initially released in the year 2005.
- *Shadowgrounds Survivor*[2] is a sequel to Shadowgrounds. It was also developed by Frozenbyte and released in 2007.
- *Trine*[3] is an action-oriented puzzle game. It was developed by Frozenbyte as well and released in 2009.

The determination of representative cloud gaming providers is somewhat challenging. Following an initial hype around cloud gaming, which resulted in a variety of new suppliers, the market appears to be in a phase of consolidation today. For example, *Gaikai*, one of the pioneers in cloud gaming, was acquired in August 2012 by the major industry player *Sony* [16], and had temporally ceased its services; recent reports indicate that Sony plans to exploit Gaikai for the delivery of games to its new *PlayStation 4* gaming console starting in the third quarter of 2014 [17]. This work includes measurements for three provisioning options:

- *Cloud Gaming Provider A* (CGP-A), which is located in the Americas and operates a dedicated infrastructure[4].
- *Cloud Gaming Provider B* (CGP-B), with headquarters in the Asian-Pacific region, which also uses a dedicated infrastructure.
- *A local personal computer* (Local), which is equipped with an Intel Core 2 Quad Q6700 CPU, an NVidia Geforce GTX 560 GPU, and 4 GB of memory.

As it has been explained before, cloud gaming employs the Internet as delivery channel. Because the network as such is out of the control sphere of both provider and user, we focus on the user's network connection in our experiments. Specifically, we regard the following techniques:

---

[1] http://www.shadowgroundsgame.com/
[2] http://www.shadowgroundssurvivor.com/
[3] http://www.trine-thegame.com/
[4] Unfortunately, due to legal considerations, we are required to anonymize the names of the cloud gaming providers.

- *Universal Mobile Telecommunications System* (UMTS), which marks the third generation (3G) of cellular networks and has been widely deployed in many industrialized countries since the mid-2000s. We use a variant with the *High Speed Packet Access* (HSPA) extensions.
- *Long Term Evolution* (LTE), which corresponds to the fourth generation (4G) of cellular networks. It has recently been or is currently being introduced by many mobile network providers.
- *Very High Speed Digital Subscriber Line* (VDSL), which denotes the cutting-edge in traditional fixed-line, copper cable-based Internet access.

2.2   Measurement Tool and Procedure

The aim of our approach is to automate the measurement process to the largest possible extent. For that matter, we have devised a GAme LAtency MEasurement TOol, or in brief, GALAMETO.KOM. This tool autonomously invokes a predefined action in the game and measures the time interval until the corresponding reaction can be observed. As a preparatory step, the tool requires the user to specify the trigger that invokes a certain action in the game. Such trigger may consist in pressing a mouse button or a key. Furthermore, the user has to specify the screen area that will reflect the corresponding reaction, such as the display of gunfire or the main menu. In order to reliably identify the reaction, the user further declares a numerical sensitivity value δ. This sensitivity value reflects the change of the *average color* within the predefined screen area. Lastly, in order to start an experiment, the user specifies the desired number of observations in the sample.

For each measurement iteration, GALAMETO.KOM first invokes the specified trigger. That is, it submits the user-defined activity to the game and stores a timestamp t_{act}. Then, the tool scans the frontbuffer of the graphics card and computes the initial average color value c_{init} for the predefined screen area. That procedure is continuously repeated, each time updating the current average color c_{curr} and a corresponding timestamp t_{react}. Once a change of color, i. e., a reaction with sufficient magnitude, is detected (i. e., if $|c_{curr} - c_{init}| \geq \delta$ holds), the latency $t_{lat} = t_{react} - t_{act}$ can be computed. The latency value is stored as new observation, and the process is repeated until a sample of the desired size has been collected.

For our experiment, we followed a so-called *full factorial design*. That is, we conducted measurements for each possible value combination of the three independent variables. Because the local execution of a single-player game is independent of the network connection, there are seven possible combinations of provider and network. For each combination, we examine the three selected games. Thus, our experimental setup consists of 21 different *test cases*.

For each test case, we acquired a sample of 250 observations. Subsequently, we checked for statistically significant differences between the test cases with respect to the mean latencies using a parametric t-test [18,19]. For validation purposes, a non-parametric Mann-Whitney U-test was additionally applied [19]. Both tests were conducted at the same confidence level of 95 % (i. e., $\alpha = 0.05$). The mean latencies of a pair of test cases are only considered significantly different if the according indication is given by both tests.

All experiments were executed using the previously specified computer in order to avoid measurement inaccuracies due to hardware differences. The different network connections were provided by a major German telecommunications provider. No artificial network disturbances were introduced into the measurement process.

2.3   Results and Discussion

The results of our experiment, i. e., observed mean latencies are illustrated in Figs. 1, 2, and 3 for the three games respectively. In addition, Table 1 contains the detailed results that have been the basis for the figures.

As can be seen, a local execution of the games yields the lowest latencies, ranging from 22 ms for Shadowgrounds to 44 ms for Trine. As it may have been expected, the latencies significantly increase with the novelty of the game. Because the remaining latency components can be assumed constant, this indicates a growth of computational complexity within the game pipeline, i. e., the overall increase in latency can likely be traced back to increased CPU and GPU time.

For cloud gaming provider A, we observe mean latencies between approximately 65 ms and 130 ms. The latencies significantly decrease with improved network connectivity. Specifically, with respect to the cellular networks, LTE is able to reduce the mean latency by up to 35 ms compared to UMTS. A fixed-line connection, namely VDSL, yields a further reduction of up to 12 ms. In general, the latency increases diminish compared to a local execution with the novelty of the game. This indicates that the latency of the game pipeline can, in fact, be reduced through the use of dedicated hardware in the cloud data center (cf. Sect. 2.1). However, the effect does not compensate for the network delay in our test cases. Hence, regardless of the game and network connection, provider A is not able to compete with a local execution in terms of latency. Depending on the network connection, cloud gaming adds between 40 ms and 90 ms of latency for each considered game. These differences are statistically significant at the assumed confidence level of 95 %.

For cloud gaming provider B, we find even higher mean latencies between about 150 ms and 220 ms. Once again, there is a significant reduction in these figures with improved network connectivity. Compared to UMTS, LTE achieves a reduction of up to 29 ms, which very similar to the results for cloud gaming provider A. Likewise, VDSL shaves off between 9 ms and 17 ms in latency in comparison to LTE. In contrast to provider A, we do not find a decreasing latency margin with increasing novelty, i. e., computational complexity, of the game. Thus, provider B is even less capable than provider A of competing with a local execution in terms of latency. Specifically, depending on the game, provider B adds between 100 ms and 150 ms of latency. As for provider A, these increases are statistically significant.

In addition, the box-and-whisker plots indicate higher variations in the observed latencies, i. e., higher jitter, for both cloud gaming providers compared to a local game execution. This is also important to note, since previous research has not only identified absolute latencies, but also high jitter as an aspect in cloud gaming systems that may substantially impair the QoE of the end user [20].

Table 1. Detailed results for the independent variable latency per test case (in ms). Abbreviations: SG – Shadowgrounds; SGS – Shadowgrounds Survivor; CI95 – Radius of the 95 % confidence interval; Pc. – Percentile.

Game	Provider	Network	Mean	CI95	2.5th Pc.	25th Pc.	Median	75th Pc.	97.5th Pc.
SG	CGP-A	UMTS	93.65	6.49	68.98	81.06	87.49	95.00	132.66
SG	CGP-A	LTE	76.39	1.34	55.04	69.74	76.65	83.19	96.76
SG	CGP-A	VDSL	64.39	0.98	48.01	59.05	64.52	69.96	79.75
SG	CGP-B	UMTS	205.34	3.00	167.71	189.81	200.33	216.11	262.00
SG	CGP-B	LTE	181.47	3.20	145.54	163.79	179.08	193.80	263.31
SG	CGP-B	VDSL	170.09	3.29	136.85	151.75	166.23	178.13	259.15
SG	Local	N/A	22.13	0.93	7.91	17.46	22.68	27.80	36.00
SGS	CGP-A	UMTS	106.19	1.61	83.63	96.21	106.89	115.02	130.41
SGS	CGP-A	LTE	80.41	1.40	60.26	72.82	79.59	87.32	102.33
SGS	CGP-A	VDSL	70.43	1.00	56.06	64.66	70.00	76.13	86.90
SGS	CGP-B	UMTS	217.63	3.27	182.11	200.11	213.73	231.18	285.12
SGS	CGP-B	LTE	201.58	2.85	161.56	189.64	198.71	210.90	261.06
SGS	CGP-B	VDSL	184.45	2.73	150.83	167.37	183.18	199.11	224.45
SGS	Local	N/A	33.79	1.11	16.64	27.69	34.03	39.98	51.08
Trine	CGP-A	UMTS	128.13	1.91	95.56	117.01	128.43	139.00	153.98
Trine	CGP-A	LTE	93.06	1.31	76.26	85.96	93.24	99.48	112.61
Trine	CGP-A	VDSL	82.88	1.25	67.05	75.82	82.03	88.62	106.85
Trine	CGP-B	UMTS	189.58	2.57	157.01	176.04	187.87	201.02	239.97
Trine	CGP-B	LTE	160.76	3.11	130.12	145.36	156.74	169.60	219.02
Trine	CGP-B	VDSL	151.69	2.01	118.01	141.79	152.10	161.56	181.86
Trine	Local	N/A	44.68	1.83	25.14	35.90	41.01	49.29	84.01

In summary, with respect to the first research question from Sect. 1, we conclude that cloud gaming has a significant and negative impact on the QoS parameter of latency, compared to the local execution of a game. Depending on the provider and network connection, cloud gaming results in latency increases between 40 ms and 150 ms. In relative terms, the increases amount to between 85 % (Trine at CGP-A using VDSL) and 828 % (Shadowgrounds at CGP-B using UMTS).

As previously explained, our focus in this work was on QoS, i. e., objective quality figures. Thus, the subjective perception of our results may substantially differ between various player groups. According to Dick et al., the mean tolerable latencies for an unimpaired experience in a multi-player game are in the range

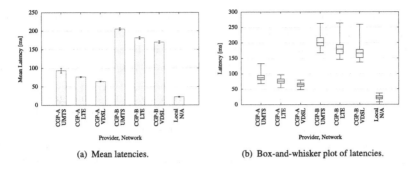

(a) Mean latencies.

(b) Box-and-whisker plot of latencies.

Fig. 1. Observed latencies for the game *Shadowgrounds* (sample size $n = 250$). In Fig. 1(a), error bars indicate the 95 % confidence intervals. In Fig. 1(b), the box marks the 25th, 50th, and 75th percentiles, and the whiskers indicate the 2.5th and 97.5th percentiles.

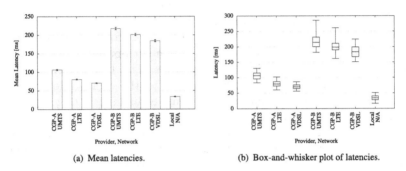

(a) Mean latencies.

(b) Box-and-whisker plot of latencies.

Fig. 2. Observed latencies for the game *Shadowgrounds Survivor* (sample size $n = 250$). Same notation as in Fig. 1.

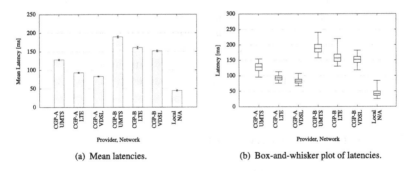

(a) Mean latencies.

(b) Box-and-whisker plot of latencies.

Fig. 3. Observed latencies for the game *Trine* (sample size $n = 250$). Same notation as in Fig. 1.

between 50 and 100 ms; maximal tolerable latencies are approximately 50 ms higher, i. e., in the order of 100 to 150 ms [10]. User studies by Jarschel et al. also indicate that the Quality of Experience (QoE) quickly drops with increasing latency, specifically in fast-paced games such as racing simulations or first-person shooters [4]. Hence, based on the observed numbers, we believe that cloud gaming is primarily attractive for slow-paced games, as well as casual players who likely have moderate QoS expectations compared to experienced and sophisticated gamers.

Given the reliance on the Internet as delivery medium, cloud gaming would likely profit from a shift away from the best-effort philosophy towards sophisticated QoS mechanisms. The development of such mechanisms has been an active field of research for many years, resulting in proposals such as *Integrated Services* (IntServ) or *Differentiated Services* (DiffServ) [21]. However, past experience – for example, with the rather sluggish introduction of *IPv6* – has shown that many Internet service providers are rather reluctant to make fundamental infrastructure changes unless a pressing need arises. In addition, as the ongoing debate about *net neutrality* shows, the introduction of QoS management techniques on the Internet is not merely a technical issue. For a more comprehensive discussion, we refer the interested reader to Xiao [22].

Assuming that the Internet itself will remain to follow a best-effort philosophy in the short and medium term, two main options remain for cloud providers to improve the QoS of their systems. The first option consists in moving the data centers geographically closer to the clients. However, for a constant client base, such decentralization implies building a larger number of data centers. Due to the reduced size and thus, smaller economies of scale of these data centers [23], such approach is likely to be cost-intensive. A viable alternative may consist in the exploitation of servers in existing content delivery networks, as proposed by Choy et al. [3]. Second, cloud providers may upgrade their servers to reduce the latency of the game pipeline. Thus, they could aim to (over-)compensate for the network latency. However, while such an approach may be successful for computationally complex games, it will likely fail for older games where the impact of the game pipeline is relatively small. In addition, server upgrades can be costly, specifically if disproportionately expensive high-end components have to be purchased. Hence, in our opinion, a key challenge for cloud providers consists in finding an economically reasonable balance between QoS (and thus, the potential number of customers) and cost.

3   Examination of Round-Trip Times Between Globally Distributed Compute Nodes

This section describes the second part of our experiments, i. e., the quantification of latencies between globally distributed compute nodes, representing fictitious cloud data centers. Similar to the previous section, we first explain the considered variables and measurement procedure, followed by a presentation and discussion of results.

3.1   Considered Variables

For this second part of our research, we conceived two linked experiments. The first examines the *bilateral* latency among different globally distributed locations in order to assess the maximum feasible distance between a provider and consumer. In contrast, the second experiment focuses on the *unilateral* latency between a single client and aforementioned compute nodes, depending on different network connections.

Similar to the previous section, latency constitutes the dependent variable in our experiments. However, in contrast to our previous experiment, we focus on a specific component of latency, namely *Round-Trip Time* (RTT), i. e., the timespan between the sending of a ping packet and receipt of the corresponding pong packet. RTT is also referred to as "network delay" in related research [13]. Since RTTs are only a part of overall latency in cloud gaming systems – cf. Sect. 2.1 – and processing times are explicitly not considered, our results should be seen as a lower bound on overall latency.

For both the bilateral and unilateral measurements, we used an identical set of 15 globally distributed compute nodes, each representing a fictitious cloud data center. For the bilateral measurements, the *source node* and *target node* constitute independent variables. In the unilateral measurements, only the latter is considered, because all measurements are taken from the identical source host. In the unilateral measurements, we further considered the client's *network connection* as independent variable. Since our experiments were conducted independent of the latency measurements from Sect. 2, we did not have access to the dedicated network connections of aforementioned telecommunications provider anymore. Hence, we used the following two options:

- *UMTS* with HSPA extensions, using the public cellular network of another major German telecommunications provider.
- *Wireless Local Area Network* (WLAN), provided by an access point that was attached to our university's high-bandwidth network.

3.2   Measurement Tool and Procedure

For the purposes of our experiment, we conceived and implemented an additional measurement utility. It uses the tool *tcping*[5] for Windows respectively a comparable script *tcpping*[6] for Linux to repeatedly measure the RTT between the respective node and all remaining nodes.

In accordance with the previous section, we also followed a *full factorial design*, conducting measurements for each distinct value combination of the independent variables. In the case of the bilateral measurements, this results in 210 test cases, each representing a specific combination of the 15 source and target nodes. For the unilateral measurements, we considered 30 test cases, each

---

[5] http://www.elifulkerson.com/projects/tcping.php
[6] http://www.vdberg.org/~richard/tcpping.html

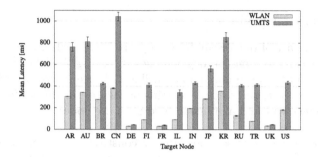

Fig. 4. Observed mean RTTs in the unilateral measurements (with 95 % confidence intervals), using clients with different connection types in Darmstadt, Germany, by target node (effective sample size $n' \geq 991$).

resulting from a distinct combination of the 15 target nodes and two network connections.

As common testbed for our experiments, we chose PlanetLab [24], a research network that consisted of approximately 1,200 globally distributed nodes at 550 sites as of January 2014[7]. We selected 15 nodes on five continents (Asia, Africa, America, Europe, Australia) to serve as fictitious cloud data centers, representing the providers of cloud-based multimedia services, and deployed our measurement utility on these nodes. The measurement utility was executed over a timespan of approximately four days, resulting in samples of 10,000 RTT observations for each pair of nodes in the bilateral measurements. For the unilateral measurements, we obtained a smaller sample of 1,000 RTT observations for each network connection and target node. For each sample, we subsequently computed the mean RTT value and corresponding 95 % confidence interval [19].

3.3   Results and Discussion

The results for the bilateral and unilateral measurements are provided in Tables 2 and 3. Furthermore, the results for the unilateral measurements are visualized in Fig. 4. Please note that timed-out pings were not considered in the computation of mean RTTs, hence resulting in differing *effective* sizes for each underlying sample.

Since the propagation of electric signals is constrained by the speed of light, it comes as little surprise that the observed latencies dramatically increase with the geographical distance between two nodes. Choy et al. [3] explain that the processing of game content on the client and server side requires approximately 20 ms. This aligns well with the overall latency of approximately 20 ms to 40 ms that we found for local gaming in the previous section and also corresponds to delays of about 30 ms that were found by Huang et al. as part of experimental studies with their GamingAnywhere system [13]. Hence, RTTs should not exceed a threshold of about 80 ms to permit for acceptable QoE.

---

[7] http://www.planet-lab.org/

Table 2. Observed mean RTTs (in ms; with 95 % confidence intervals) between pairs of globally distributed nodes (effective sample size $n' \geq 9,490$).

		Target Node														
		AR	AU	BR	CN	DE	FI	FR	IL	IN	JP	KR	RU	TR	UK	US
Source Node	AR	-	360.4	80.7	360.2	333.5	348.7	310.6	369.7	512.0	435.6	422.8	346.0	374.8	314.8	211.9
		-	(0.3)	(0.3)	(0.3)	(0.3)	(0.2)	(0.4)	(0.3)	(0.3)	(0.3)	(0.7)	(0.3)	(0.4)	(0.3)	(0.4)
	AU	360.9	-	367.9	269.5	356.0	374.1	333.0	392.1	300.2	296.2	295.0	349.6	397.5	337.4	198.3
		(0.4)	-	(0.3)	(0.1)	(0.0)	(0.1)	(0.1)	(0.0)	(0.8)	(0.0)	(0.1)	(0.5)	(0.1)	(0.0)	(0.6)
	BR	89.0	366.7	-	378.8	268.8	303.4	246.8	305.2	473.9	342.0	401.9	325.1	311.7	250.4	198.1
		(0.7)	(0.2)	-	(0.3)	(0.0)	(0.1)	(0.2)	(0.0)	(0.3)	(0.2)	(0.7)	(0.4)	(0.1)	(0.1)	(0.4)
	CN	364.0	269.7	384.3	-	199.6	308.5	185.1	233.4	434.0	98.0	530.2	306.8	238.6	178.7	191.1
		(0.4)	(0.1)	(0.3)	-	(0.3)	(0.2)	(0.4)	(0.4)	(3.7)	(0.4)	(5.1)	(0.6)	(0.3)	(0.4)	(0.3)
	DE	337.2	356.0	269.1	200.3	-	62.1	31.3	81.8	211.4	271.3	341.9	61.8	55.3	27.1	145.4
		(0.5)	(0.0)	(0.0)	(0.3)	-	(0.0)	(0.1)	(0.0)	(0.1)	(0.2)	(0.5)	(0.3)	(0.1)	(0.0)	(0.6)
	FI	350.7	376.7	304.4	307.9	62.1	-	76.9	120.2	268.6	308.6	341.6	55.7	97.9	65.4	186.3
		(0.3)	(0.1)	(0.1)	(0.2)	(0.0)	-	(0.1)	(0.0)	(0.2)	(0.1)	(0.1)	(0.3)	(0.1)	(0.0)	(0.2)
	FR	313.9	332.7	245.4	185.4	30.6	76.7	-	66.9	189.5	271.5	289.5	69.0	72.5	11.9	154.3
		(0.5)	(0.1)	(0.2)	(0.4)	(0.1)	(0.1)	-	(0.1)	(0.1)	(0.2)	(0.2)	(0.6)	(0.1)	(0.1)	(1.1)
	IL	372.7	392.3	305.3	233.9	81.9	120.2	67.1	-	247.6	316.2	365.1	125.2	128.0	60.4	198.4
		(0.5)	(0.0)	(0.0)	(0.4)	(0.0)	(0.0)	(0.1)	-	(0.1)	(0.2)	(0.5)	(0.6)	(0.1)	(0.0)	(0.2)
	IN	504.3	309.0	470.4	430.6	214.2	266.2	192.5	250.8	-	180.9	321.1	235.5	256.5	194.6	330.5
		(0.3)	(0.8)	(0.3)	(3.7)	(0.1)	(0.2)	(0.2)	(0.1)	-	(0.2)	(0.9)	(0.4)	(0.2)	(0.1)	(0.2)
	JP	436.2	296.2	341.6	97.9	271.1	311.0	271.9	315.9	176.3	-	37.0	301.4	306.8	261.0	155.2
		(0.4)	(0.0)	(0.3)	(0.4)	(0.2)	(0.2)	(0.2)	(0.2)	(0.1)	-	(0.0)	(0.6)	(0.2)	(0.2)	(0.7)
	KR	424.2	293.9	399.5	506.7	347.8	341.9	292.0	375.5	320.6	37.4	-	328.4	356.4	285.2	191.5
		(0.7)	(0.1)	(0.6)	(4.9)	(0.4)	(0.1)	(0.3)	(0.5)	(0.6)	(0.0)	-	(0.5)	(0.3)	(0.2)	(0.5)
	RU	349.0	345.7	324.5	301.0	59.7	54.2	67.5	122.6	233.5	299.5	328.7	-	114.9	59.1	182.4
		(0.4)	(0.3)	(0.3)	(0.4)	(0.2)	(0.2)	(0.4)	(0.4)	(0.3)	(0.3)	(0.4)	-	(0.4)	(0.4)	(0.6)
	TR	384.3	399.7	311.6	239.1	56.7	99.3	75.3	129.4	256.9	308.1	355.3	115.2	-	67.7	181.8
		(0.7)	(0.1)	(0.1)	(0.2)	(0.1)	(0.1)	(0.2)	(0.1)	(0.2)	(0.2)	(0.3)	(0.4)	-	(0.1)	(0.2)
	UK	318.4	337.4	250.5	178.6	27.1	65.4	12.0	60.4	193.0	261.4	276.1	61.9	66.5	-	144.1
		(0.5)	(0.0)	(0.0)	(0.4)	(0.0)	(0.0)	(0.1)	(0.0)	(0.1)	(0.2)	(0.1)	(0.6)	(0.1)	-	(0.5)
	US	218.0	197.9	199.3	190.4	144.8	188.8	152.2	198.3	325.5	154.1	193.2	185.7	180.4	143.6	-
		(0.4)	(0.1)	(0.4)	(0.1)	(0.1)	(0.1)	(0.2)	(0.2)	(0.1)	(0.1)	(0.3)	(0.6)	(0.2)	(0.2)	-

Table 3. Observed mean RTTs (in ms; with 95 % confidence intervals) between clients in Darmstadt (Germany), which used different Internet connection types, and globally distributed target nodes (effective sample size $n' \geq 991$).

		Target Node														
		AR	AU	BR	CN	DE	FI	FR	IL	IN	JP	KR	RU	TR	UK	US
Conn.	WLAN	303.4	341.4	276.6	380.4	30.7	90.9	30.5	91.8	194.1	282.8	354.8	128.1	77.5	35.1	182.9
		(0.9)	(0.6)	(0.4)	(3.4)	(0.4)	(0.2)	(0.4)	(0.3)	(0.7)	(1.7)	(0.4)	(3.2)	(0.4)	(0.6)	(1.5)
	UMTS	761.4	810.2	424.2	1043.1	44.6	410.3	41.0	342.2	427.6	562.5	853.1	405.9	412.1	47.0	433.6
		(40.8)	(42.5)	(11.9)	(41.0)	(1.1)	(18.3)	(2.9)	(24.8)	(12.3)	(27.2)	(43.2)	(10.9)	(11.5)	(2.6)	(14.1)

This argument confirms our statement from Sect. 2.3 that cloud data centers for the provision of cloud gaming services should be placed in geographical proximity to the potential clients. Specifically, the results for the bilateral measurements from Table 2 indicate the such proximity more or less translates into placement on the same continent. For example, RTTs between Argentina (AR) and Brazil (BR), or Germany (DE) and Finland (FI) were found to fairly accurately meet the aforementioned threshold of 80 ms.

This observation is underpinned by the results of the unilateral measurements in Table 3. Specifically in UMTS networks, the observed RTT drastically increases with geographical distance and easily exceeds the acceptable threshold, even for target nodes that were placed close to our client in Darmstadt, Germany, e.g., in Finland (FI) or Israel (IL). Furthermore, the results indicate that the gap in RTT between UMTS and WLAN is statistically significant at the assumed confidence level of 95 % and quickly widens with geographical distance. For example, for the Western European target hosts, such as Germany (DE), France (FR), or the United Kingdom (UK), we observed relative moderate absolute increases of 10 ms to 15 ms, or less than 50 % in relative terms. In contrast, geographically more remote locations, such as Turkey (TR) or Israel (IL), were found to provide an acceptable latency around 80 ms when using WLAN, while the mean RTTs increase to more than 300 ms in UMTS networks.

In summary, with respect to the second research question from Sect. 1, we conclude that the placement of data centers close to the potential customers is a key factor in providing cloud gaming services with adequate QoS properties. Furthermore, the work at hand shows that not only WLAN, but also UMTS cellular networks may allow for cloud-based gaming if the cloud data centers that provide the according services are placed in geographical proximity to the user.

4 Related Work

Chen et al. have, to the best of our knowledge, been the first to conduct empirical latency measurements of actual cloud gaming providers [8]. In their experiments, they regarded *OnLive*, a commercial provider, as well as, *StreamMyGame*, a free software tool that permits to set up a private video game stream. Chen et al. propose and implement a measurement tool which is based on similar conceptual ideas as GALAMETO.KOM. Most notably, the authors also trigger a certain action – in their case, the invocation of the in-game menu – and observe the appearance of the corresponding reaction based on color changes. In their experiments, they find streaming delays – which do not include the network latency – between 135 ms and 240 ms for OnLive and up to 500 ms for StreamMyGame. Thus, their results are in a similar order of magnitude as the values that have been observed in our experiments. In contrast to this work, Chen et al. trigger the comparison process in the measurement tool through a redirected Direct3D function call and operate on the backbuffer of the graphics card, not the frontbuffer. Thus, the latency component that is introduced through the copying of the backbuffer scene into the frontbuffer has not been considered in their work. In addition, and more importantly, the authors do not use a locally executed game as benchmark in their experiments.

Jarschel et al. have conducted a user-study involving 58 participants on QoE of cloud gaming depending on network characteristics [4]. For that purpose, they generate an audio/video stream using a *PlayStation 3* gaming console. This stream is subjected to artificial delay and packet loss, ranging between 0 and 300 ms and 0 and 1 % respectively, in different test scenarios. Jarschel et al. find that the quality of the downstream, i. e., the link between provider and user, has a substantially higher impact on the QoE than the quality of the upstream, i. e., the link between user and provider. Their results also indicate that packet loss is of higher relevance than latency for the subjective quality perception. The main difference compared to our work consists in the focus on subjective, rather than objective quality aspects. In addition, Jarschel et al. did not regard commercial cloud providers in their experiments.

Wang and Dey have proposed a cloud gaming system for mobile clients called *Cloud Mobile Gaming* (CMG) [25]. As part of their work, they examine the impact of different factors on the user experience. The considered factors involve the video stream configuration and quality, the game configuration, delay (i. e., latency), and packet loss. Similarly to Jarschel et al., the authors use a controlled experimental setup, in which they systematically vary the values of the previously mentioned factors. Using a study group of 21 participants, they infer impairment functions for these factors. The findings are subsequently validated using a control group of 15 participants. Based on practical measurements, the authors conclude that their CMG system may provide a subjectively good or mediocre gaming experience in WLAN and cellular networks, respectively. In contrast to our work, which considers public cloud gaming providers and the local execution of games, Wang and Dey exclusively examine their own, proprietary cloud gaming system.

Outside the academic world, West has measured the latency of various locally executed games on a PlayStation 3 console [26]. West uses a commodity digital camera in order to take high-frequency photographs of the game controller and the attached screen during gameplay. Based on a subsequent manual analysis of the resulting picture stream, he deduces the timespan between a button press and the corresponding action. West finds latencies between approximately 50 ms and 300 ms on the PlayStation 3. The main benefit ob West's method is the clear separation between the gaming system and the measurement system. In addition, the camera-based approach also permits to capture the LCD response time. However, the accuracy of the measurement is limited by the maximal framerate of the camera. In addition, GALAMETO.KOM only requires a brief preparatory manual tuning phase, whereas West's method requires substantial manual effort, which renders the collection of large data samples difficult.

Continuous measurements of latencies among various geographically distributed nodes are carried out within the so-called *Ping End-to-end Reporting* (PingER)[8] project. The project – which was started in 1995 and involves more than 700 worldwide nodes today – publicly provides its results in various formats through its Web site. Unfortunately, the project focuses on bilateral measurements and does not provide data on different network connections, such as cellular and wireless networks.

An open-source cloud gaming system, called *GamingAnywhere*, has been proposed by Huang et al. [13]. The software is available for public download through the project's Web site[9]. Huang et al. examine the performance of their system with respect to QoS and QoE properties through an experimental evaluation, based on three different games, and compare it to the performance of a commercial cloud gaming provider, namely OnLive, and a similar system, namely StreamMyGame. The authors find that their system provides latencies of around 40 ms to 45 ms, compared to about 150 ms to 200 ms for OnLive and approximately 400 ms for StreamMyGame. Based on their experiments, Huang et al.

---

[8] http://www-iepm.slac.stanford.edu/pinger/
[9] http://gaminganywhere.org/

also claim that GamingAnywhere incurs substantially lower network load and features higher video quality than the two other systems. In contrast to our work, their paper does not include a comparison with local gaming and does not feature RTT measurements for globally distributed data centers.

In our recent work [12], we have identified latency, energy consumption, and cost as main challenges for *mobile* cloud gaming. Similar to the work at hand, this previous publication provided unilateral RTT measurements in cellular and wireless networks. However, it did not feature large-scale bilateral measurements between globally distributed compute nodes, and did not consider actual cloud gaming providers.

Lastly, this invited paper builds on and extends our own previous publication [27]. As major novel contribution, the work at hand features bilateral and unilateral RTT measurements, which are a valuable complement to the primary experiment that focused on latency in cloud-based and local gaming.

5   Summary and Conclusions

The cloud computing paradigm has substantially transformed the delivery of IT services. A relatively new service class within this context is cloud gaming. In cloud gaming, video games are centrally executed in a cloud data center and delivered to the customer as an audio/video stream via the Internet. While this model has many advantages both from a user and provider perspective, it also introduces the Internet into the delivery chain, which may inflict the Quality of Service for the user.

In this work, our first focus was on the experimental evaluation of user-perceived latency in cloud-based and locally executed video games. For that matter, we created the semi-automatic measurement tool GALAMETO.KOM. We conducted latency measurement for two cloud gaming providers, using three different games and network types, respectively. Our results indicate that cloud gaming exhibits significantly higher latency than a local execution. Absolute increases were in the range between 40 ms and 150 ms, while the relative increases approximately amounted to between 85 % and 800 %. The margin between cloud providers and the local execution diminished with an improved network connection and an increase in computational complexity of the game.

As a complement to our primary experiment, this work featured an assessment of round-trip times among globally distributed compute nodes, as well as between these nodes and a single client that used different network connections. Here, we found mean round-trip times between 10 ms and 530 ms and 40 ms and 1050 ms for the first and second setup, respectively. These results confirm the notion that the provision of cloud games with adequate QoS properties require a placement of cloud data centers in geographical proximity to end users, specifically if cellular networks are used as delivery medium.

References

1. Dikaiakos, M., Katsaros, D., Mehra, P., Pallis, G., Vakali, A.: Cloud computing: distributed internet computing for IT and scientific research. IEEE Internet Comput. **13**, 10–13 (2009)
2. Buyya, R., Yeo, C., Venugopal, S., Broberg, J., Brandic, I.: Cloud computing and emerging IT platforms: vision, hype, and reality for delivering computing as the 5th utility. Future Gener. Comput. Syst. **25**, 599–616 (2009)
3. Choy, S., Wong, B., Simon, G., Rosenberg, C.: The brewing storm in cloud gaming: a measurement study on cloud to end-user latency. In: 11th Annual Workshop on Network and Systems Support for Games (2012)
4. Jarschel, M., Schlosser, D., Scheuring, S., Hossfeld, T.: An evaluation of QoE in cloud gaming based on subjective tests. In: 5th International Conference on Innovative Mobile and Internet Services in Ubiquitous Computing (2011)
5. Ross, P.: Cloud computing's killer app: gaming. IEEE Spect. **46**, 14 (2009)
6. Süselbeck, R., Schiele, G., Becker, C.: Peer-to-peer support for low-latency massively multiplayer online games in the cloud. In: 8th Annual Workshop on Network and Systems Support for Games (2009)
7. Mell, P., Grance, T.: The NIST definition of cloud computing - special publication 800–145. Technical report, National Institute of Standards and Technology (2011)
8. Chen, K., Chang, Y., Tseng, P., Huang, C., Lei, C.: Measuring the latency of cloud gaming systems. In: 19th ACM International Conference on Multimedia (2011)
9. Courcoubetis, C., Dramitinos, M., Stamoulis, G., Blocq, G., Miron, A., Orda, A.: Inter-carrier interconnection services: QoS, economics and business issues. In: 2011 IEEE Symposium on Computers and Communications (2011)
10. Dick, M., Wellnitz, O., Wolf, L.: Analysis of factors affecting players' performance and perception in multiplayer games. In: 4th ACM SIGCOMM Workshop on Network and System Support for Games (2005)
11. Claypool, M., Claypool, K.: Latency can kill: precision and deadline in online games. In: First Annual ACM SIGMM Conference on Multimedia Systems (2010)
12. Lampe, U., Hans, R., Steinmetz, R.: Will mobile cloud gaming work? findings on latency, energy, and cost. In: 2nd International Conference on Mobile Services (2013)
13. Huang, C.Y., Hsu, C.H., Chang, Y.C., Chen, K.T.: GamingAnywhere: an open cloud gaming system. In: 4th Multimedia Systems Conference (2013)
14. Wang, J.: NVIDIA GeForce GRID - A Glimpse at the Future of Gaming (2012). http://www.geforce.com/whats-new/articles/geforce-grid
15. Wilson, D.: Exploring Input Lag Inside and Out (2009). http://www.anandtech.com/show/2803/7
16. Gaikai: Gaikai.com : History (2013). http://www.gaikai.com/history
17. Orland, K.: Report: Gaikai Streaming Coming to PS4 in Third Quarter of 2014 — Ars Technica (2013). http://arstechnica.com/gaming/2013/12/report-gaikai-streaming-coming-to-ps4-in-third-quarter-of-2014/
18. Jain, R.K.: The Art of Computer Systems Performance Analysis: Techniques for Experimental Design, Measurement, Simulation, and Modeling. Wiley, New York (1991)
19. Kirk, R.: Statistics: An Introduction, 5th edn. Wadsworth Publishing, Belmont (2007)
20. Cai, W., Leung, V.: Multiplayer cloud gaming system with cooperative video sharing. In: 4th International Conference on Cloud Computing Technology and Science (2012)

21. Tanenbaum, A.S.: Computer Networks, 4th edn. Pearson Education, Singapore (2003)
22. Xiao, X.: Technical, Commercial and Regulatory Challenges of QoS: An Internet Service Model Perspective. Morgan Kaufmann, San Francisco (2008)
23. Greenberg, A., Hamilton, J., Maltz, D., Patel, P.: The cost of a cloud: research problems in data center networks. ACM SIGCOMM Comput. Commun. Rev. **39**, 68–73 (2008)
24. Chun, B., Culler, D., Roscoe, T., Bavier, A., Peterson, L., Wawrzoniak, M., Bowman, M.: PlanetLab: an overlay testbed for broad-coverage services. ACM SIGCOMM Comput. Commun. Rev. **33**, 3–12 (2003)
25. Wang, S., Dey, S.: Modeling and characterizing user experience in a cloud server based mobile gaming approach. In: 2009 IEEE Global Telecommunications Conference (2009)
26. West, M.: Measuring Responsiveness in Video Games (2008). http://www.gamasutra.com/view/feature/132122/measuring_responsiveness_in_video_.php
27. Lampe, U., Wu, Q., Hans, R., Miede, A., Steinmetz, R.: To frag or to be fragged - an empirical assessment of latency in cloud gaming. In: 3rd International Conference on Cloud Computing and Services Science (2013)

Multi-dimensional Model Driven Policy Generation

Juan Li[✉], Wendpanga Francis Ouedraogo, and Frédérique Biennier

Université de Lyon, CNRS INSA-Lyon, LIRIS UMR 5205,
20 Avenue Albert Einstein 69621, 69621 Villeurbanne Cedex, France
{juan.li,wendpanga-francis.ouedraogo,
frederique.biennier}@liris.cnrs.fr

Abstract. As Cloud Computing provides agile and scalable IT infrastructure, QoS-assured services and customizable computing environment, it increases the call for agile and dynamic deployment and governance environments over multi-cloud infrastructure. By now, governance and Non Functional Properties (such as security, QoS...) are managed in a static way, limiting the global benefits of deploying service-based information system over multi-cloud environments. To overcome this limit, we propose a contextualised policy generation process to allow both an agile management NFP in a multi-cloud context and a secured deployment of the service-based information system. The last step of this Model Driven Policy Engineering approach uses policies as Model@runtime to select, compose, deploy and orchestrate NFP management functions depending on the exact execution context. Moreover, a dynamic governance loop including autonomic KPI management is used to control continuously the governance results.

Keywords: Multi-Cloud governance · Policy generation · Model driven engineering · NFP management · Security

1 Introduction

Cloud Computing is transforming the way enterprises purchase and manage computing resources [1], increasing corporate information System robustness and scalability. This organisation also fits the collaborative business stake as collaborative business processes are distributed among different IS and clouds. According to a "cloud provider vision", this leads to different challenges: managing virtual services instances, workload segmentation and portability, automating the service provisioning while optimizing use of the resources and accelerating the deployment of new services [2]. These challenges increase the call for a common cloud service reference architecture, enabling cloud portability and cloud service governance. As far as the "cloud consumer" vision is concerned, the (multi-)cloud strategy adoption increases the call for developing agile and secured deployment means so that the target cloud characteristics can be taken into account in a transparent way. Several works (presented in the related works section) cope partly with these agile and secured deployment and governance challenges, either related to the "technical" side of the multi-cloud system or related to a "Business" vision.

© Springer International Publishing Switzerland 2014
M. Helfert et al. (Eds.): CLOSER 2013, CCIS 453, pp. 69–85, 2014.
DOI: 10.1007/978-3-319-11561-0_5

Nevertheless none of them integrate a "transverse" vision from business to technical implementation. To overcome this limit, we propose to federate the business and cloud vision in a single model-driven approach to generate policies related to Non Functional Properties management. Then in a "model at runtime" vision these policies are used to orchestrate contextually the management/security/governance services at runtime.

2 State of the Art

As defined by [3], Cloud Computing enables convenient, on-demand network access to a shared pool of configurable computing resources that can be rapidly provisioned and released with minimal management effort or service provider interaction. To tune the deployment process depending on the cloud characteristics, one can use the 2-dimension typology introduced by [4]:

- **The Service Dimension** (which refers to the common XaaS vision) is used to split the cloud offer into 4 layers (hardware/data center, Infrastructure as a service layer, Platform as a Service layer and Application/Software as a Service layer) that may even be "enriched" with a Business Process as a Service layer.
- **The Deployment Model Dimension** which depends on who owns and who uses the cloud resources leading to classify cloud resources as Public, Private, Community or Hybrid clouds which mix public and private resources.

Unfortunately, this model does not really integrate a business vision. Moreover, the deployment model is often defined in a static way so that QoS or security management can not be adapted dynamically depending on the real execution context (Fig. 1).

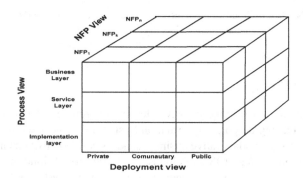

Fig. 1. Governance Multi-dimensional model.

2.1 Adapting QoS Management and Governance to Multi-cloud Systems

As stated in [5], users increase their call for functionalities that automate the management of services as a whole unit, from the business to the infrastructure layer. To this end [6] provides a formal model to express visibility constraints, manage compliance and configure cloud resources on demand. Nevertheless, this model is defined according to a static execution context and does not support dynamic reconfiguration at runtime. To overcome this limit and allow a fine-grain tuning of resources, specification at the IaaS layer must integrate both computational and network constraints while adjusting the delivered infrastructure components to the users' requirements and SLAs. Nevertheless, pricing models used to this end do not integrate QoS assurance [7]. Moreover, some low-level scalability rules, such as VMs adjustment [8] must be integrated in a larger QoS management vision as application consolidation processes (used to increase resource utilization) should take into account the performance interference of co-located workloads to fit the application required QoS [9]. Lastly, a particular attention must be paid on the way "elastic QoS" is defined in order to avoid penalties due to the risk of deviation from the agreed QoS level [10] scalability. On the opposite, higher-level approaches fail to provide mechanisms for a fine grained control of services at runtime [11]. This increases the call for a global governance system allowing an efficient execution and support of collaborative business processes, without wastes and cause of defect.

This requirement involves monitoring both infrastructure and services, taking into account SLAs, elasticity, QoS, etc. [12]. As trust, managerial capability and technical capability have a significant relationship with cloud-deployment performance [13], SLAs should be understood by both cloud experts and non-experts so that common performance indicators can be recognised. Unfortunately, as stated in [14], SLA frameworks are focused on technical attributes and do neither take into account security nor other business related non-functional properties. Moreover, resources measuring techniques need further refinement to be applied in the cloud context in order (1) to ensure some level of trust between service providers and customers, (2) to provide a flexible and agile way to tune performance metrics parameters and (3) to support real costs evaluation means.

To this end, [15] proposes a self-adaptive hierarchical monitoring mechanism for clouds. Implemented at the Platform as a Service layer, it allows monitoring the QoS parameters based on SLA for business benefits. Nevertheless it lacks of providing a flexible policy enforcement mechanism and it does not indicate its scalability in web service framework. While considering quality from a "customer" point of view, [16] proposes a comprehensive quality model for service-oriented systems, determining the dependency value and ranking the quality priority. However, the performance issues related to cloud resources are not discussed and details are missing regarding the correlation of the quality model with the service cost model.

Lastly, the monitoring mechanisms should be non-intrusive and should let a minimum runtime footprint over the execution environment [11]. It has also (1) to fit the cloud elasticity to keep up when an application or infrastructure scales up or down dynamically [18] and (2) to provide a "simple" interface so that the cloud complexity is as transparent as possible for end users. This requires being able to "generate and deploy on the fly" contextual monitoring means.

2.2   Integration of Security Management

Due to the variety of cloud deployment models, different security challenges must be taken into account. While private Cloud deployment does not require to enforce the corporate security policy, the openness involved by the other kinds of deployment involves paying attention to data isolation and to data storage protection so that the corporate security policy can cope the particular vulnerabilities involved by the cloud deployment [19]. To fit these security challenges, cloud security-oriented models have also been defined such as the Cloud Security Alliance security stack [20] uses the XaaS levels to identify threats and mitigation means or the Jericho Forum Security Cube model [21]. This last model uses a 4 criteria classification: (resources physical location, the resource provider, the cloud technology and the operating area) to evaluate the risks and propose the associated mitigation means. Nevertheless, both models are organised to identify and deploy security countermeasures in a static vision and do not fit an "adaptive" security deployment in a multi-cloud context. This often leads either to "over-protect" information systems (that may reduce the Quality of Service) or to "forget" protecting corporate assets while transferring them on a cloud platform.

In order to overcome this limit, one can adapt the Model Driven Engineering (MDE) approach as its transformation steps may include platform-dependant models [22] while automating software development [23]. Such an engineering strategy can be worthy used in a multi-cloud context as it can improve reusing abilities of requirements, Platform Independent Models and parts of Platform specific models depending on the deployment platform (see for example [24]). Moreover, MDE has also been adapted to define the Model Driven Security (MDS) strategy [25, 26]. MDS can be used to generate security policies out of annotated business process models [27, 28] according to either UML based security model integration [29] or BPMN annotations [30]. Nevertheless, this approach does not allow generating and deploying automatically the convenient monitoring functions that are necessary to guaranty that the system is safe [31].

2.3 Challenges

Taking advantage of the multi-cloud deployment to support collaborative business requires integrating a unified approach to deploy secured BP and govern performances and security from the business to the infrastructure in a dynamic way. This requires first to enrich the traditional XaaS layer model with a "Business as a Service" level, used to express business-dependent non-functional requirements. Then, to fit the dynamicity required by a multi-cloud deployment, transformation models should also integrate a "model at runtime" vision to support the necessary flexibility. By now, the different works do not cover these requirements nor are end-user oriented (so that requirements can be captured more easily). To overcome these limits, we propose to take advantage of the MDE strategy to generate and deploy service-related policies that will be used to take into account non-functional requirements (as security and quality of service) while deploying and monitoring service oriented systems over a multi-cloud infrastructure.

3   Model Driven Policy Generation Process

To support the policy generation process allowing an agile management Non Functional Properties (NFP) in a multi-cloud context, we couple the MDE to the Pattern based engineering to generate service-related non-functional policies. These policies will be used at runtime to select, compose and orchestrate convenient monitoring/ security/governance services depending on the real execution context. To achieve this goal, we propose a formal model, "weaving" business and deployment environment knowledge to set transformation patterns, generate and compose NFP related policies.

3.1 Global Architecture

Our multi-dimensional model consists in different view:

- **The Process View** allows defining Business Requirements and designing the process workflow that is used to select and compose services to achieve each task. Accordingly, services are also used to select and orchestrate lower level components. This leads us to organize this view as a 3-layer architecture on the top of the XaaS model:

  - *Business Layer* (BL) includes all business context information, such as business deciders, business requirements used to identify the Business Process workflow...
  - *Service Layer* (SL) includes all virtualized service context information, such as service provider/consumer/register and includes all the services that are selected and compose to achieve a business task.
  - *Implementation Layer* (IL) includes all implementation components, such as hardware, equipments, human resources and XaaS resources etc. It contains all the components that must be composed and orchestrated to support a service execution. It is an abstraction level of the different XaaS components.

- **The Deployment View** allows defining in which kind of cloud (private, public, community or a mix of them) the process will be deployed.
- **The NFP View** is composed of a set of NFP such as security, QoS properties...

Weaving the process view and the NFP view allows to define for each activity or process, the NFP that must be governex whereas weaving the deployment view with the NFP view allows to identify how the NFP will be governed depending on the deployment context.

Our governance architecture has been designed in a "transversal" way on this architecture in a Governance as a Service strategy [32]. Governance services are composed and orchestrated while running the business processes depending on the NFP management requirements. It takes advantage of the "functional knowledge" to select, compose and orchestrate the NFP management components accordingly. This provides a rather non-intrusive system that minimizes its footprint by transforming and composing policy rules depending on the context thanks to a set of transformation patterns.

To support non functional requirements elicitation, interdependencies and clustering identification, our governance solution takes into account the business functional organization and oraganises monitoring and computing processes accordingly. Therefore it allows governance elements to be composed and orchestrated while running the business processes and allows governance execution and adaption actions fit business goals. Non-functional properties are split into different groups according to business requirements. Each group can be divided into more detailed sub-groups (according to governance needs). In our work, we focus on the most used Non Functional Properties from performance, maintainability, cost and security aspects. We classify them into four groups according to business needs. Performance group focuses on availability rate, delay rate which consists in response delay and execution delay rates, response and execution time. Maintainability group focuses on reputation, reliability, usability and accuracy. Cost group focuses on price. Security group focuses on non-reputation, confidentiality and integrity. Lastly, each group and sub-group is associated to Critical Success Factor sets. These CSF are associated to metrics used to constrain and/or evaluate their accomplishment. All required Non Functional Properties are defined in Governance Agreements, constraining associated resources (Fig. 2).

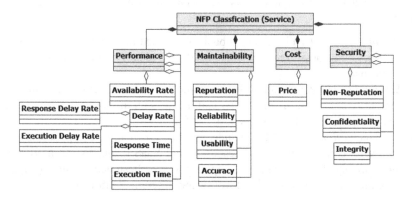

Fig. 2. Non Functional Property Taxonomy.

To allow a dynamic deployment and orchestration of the NFP management components, we propose to couple NFP related policy rules to the different functional components. Using a pattern-based transformation process, requirements are turned into Platform Independent Policies and Platform Dependant Policies used to orchestrate the NFP management components at runtime. Moreover, we take advantage of the functional specification (i.e. the BP workflow description used to compose and orchestrate the different services and cloud components) to compose and orchestrate the NFP policies deployment, monitoring and governance accordingly (Fig. 3).

The policy generation process takes advantage of both Model Driven Engineering and of Pattern-based Engineering approaches extending the works dedicated to the security non functional property such as the Model Driven Security approach or the security patterns [33, 34] to the other NFP groups.

The transformation strategy relies on a global model that connects business workflow, security and governance requirements to monitoring patterns and policies. A 'Resource' is associated either to a 'task', a 'service' or an 'implementation' component. Each resource has its own properties and interacts with others depending on the business workflow. NFP requirements (either related to security or governance) are associated to resources. Each requirement is analysed and transformed into policy rules

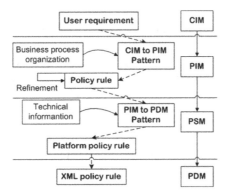

Fig. 3. Policy transformation steps.

thanks to 'transformation pattern'. Then, these policy rules are used as "Model@run-time" to select and compose security patterns, monitoring patterns or "action engines" according to the execution context and lastly orchestrate and invoke the real services that implement these patterns on the execution platform. By this way the business workflow can be secured and governed contextually (Fig. 4).

3.2   Formal Model Description

Our policy transformation process is based on a formal model integrating requirements, patterns and policy so that policy rules can be designed and transformed in a generic way.

Formally, a Requirement i is defined as a tuple:

$$Req_i = (RR, (RT, RM), RG, RL, RC) \text{ Where} \tag{1}$$

- **RR** (Requirement Resource) defines the resource concerned by the requirement. It can be a task (business activity), a service or a part of the infrastructure/piece of data.
- **RT** (Requirement Type) defines the type of the requirement (governance of one of the NFP group, ensure security, support QoS control…)
- **RG** (Requirement Goal) defines precisely the goal of this requirement (governance or other functional requirement related to a NFP)
- **RM** (Requirement Metrics) is the metric (specifically defined or standardized) to measure this requirement's implementation.
- **RL** (Requirement Layer) defines the layer (BL/SL/IL) associated to the resource targeted by this requirement.
- **RC** (Requirement context) the condition of this requirement's implementation. Such as, association of involved resource's with other resources in business workflow.
- "i" is the requirement number and "Ni" is the total number of requirements of resource Rk.

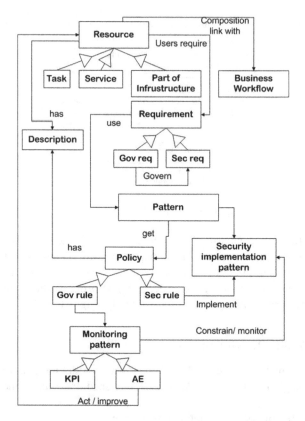

Fig. 4. Global model.

A pattern $_j$ is defined as a tuple:

$$\mathrm{Pat_j=(PatN,PatG,\{PatCtx\},PatP,\{PatCol\},\{PatR\},\{PatCsq,PatStep\})where} \quad (2)$$

- **PatN** is the name which identifies the pattern. This name is related to the requirement type, a NFP identification or or a CSF for a group of NFP.
- **PatG** defines the pattern goal (or the reason for using it). This goal is similar to the requirement goal and the associated value can be either governance or any other functional requirement related to a NFP or CSF.
- **PatCtx** identifies the context under which which this pattern can be used.
- **PatP** defines a list of "participants" and their roles in the pattern definition. A participant can refer to requirement which need to be transformed, transformed policy rule, relevant sub-pattern, collaborative business process organization, etc.
- **PatCol** describes the collaboration strategy used by the participants to interact with each other.
- **PatR** a set of related patterns. For example, governance requirement pattern requires a set of the CSF pattern for a parent NFP group pattern.)

- **PatCsq** describes the results or actions implemented by the pattern.
- **PatStep** defines the transformation step (CIM to PIM, PIM to PSM or PSM to PDM) for which the pattern must be used.
- "j" is the pattern number and "Nj" the total number of patterns.

In a similar way, a policy rule x is also defined as a tuple:

$$PolRx = (PR, PT, PG, PL, \{PC\}, PP) \text{ where} \tag{3}$$

- **PR** is the set of resources involved in the policy.
- **PT** is the Policy type. It refers to the requirement type and Pattern Name (RT and PatN) as well, as to the NFP group or the CSFs for a parent NFP group)
- **PG** defines the Policy goal and is related to RG and PatG such as governance or any other functional goal related to the NFP.
- **PL** is the layer of the involved resource for this policy. As we defined before it could be BL/SL/IL.
- **PC** is the set of conditions to decide if the policy can be used or not. (For governance policy rule, it is related to business process and organization of business workflow)
- **PP** identifies the pattern to use to define the policy implementation.
- "x" is the policy rule number.

Lastly, policy rules attached to any resource R_k can be defined by selecting (σ) the policy rules in the PolRs while the policy resource (PR) matches with resource R_k:

$$PolRs(R_k) = \sigma(PolRs.PR = R_k) (PolRs); \tag{4}$$

3.3 From Requirements to Policy Rules

At the beginning of the process, users define their requirements using a rather high abstraction level and do not have to provide any implementation technical details. As NFP management requirements are mostly specified at the Business layer, we use the "functional composition process" knowledge to select the resources belonging to the lower-levels and involved in the BL resource deployment and to propagate these requirements to these SL and IL resources. Our CIM elicitation process is based on this "composition-based" propagation models.

As stated in our formal model (see Eq. 1), each requirement is defined by specifying the resource (RR) to which this requirement is associated to and the layer to which this resource belongs as well as the type of requirement (RT), its goal (RG) and the associated metric (RM). As a resource R_k ('k' is numbering the resource) can be associated to many requirements, the Computer Independent Model is defined as the set of requirements associated to the different resources:

$$Reqs = \{Reqs (R_k)\} \text{ where} 0 < i < Ni, 0 < k < Nk \tag{5}$$

Where 'i' is the requirement number, 'Ni' is the total number of requirements associated to the resource R_k.

After gathering and formatting the requirements in a single Computer Independent Model, the policy generation process consists in turning each CIM assertion in a Platform Independent policy rule. Basic policy rules are generated thanks to a pattern-based transformation process. Our NFP classification is used to organize transformation patterns depending on the NFP they are related to. Pattern's name (PatN) and patterns' goal (PatG) are used to identify each pattern.

For each resource, the requirements are turned one after the other in a policy rule. To this end, for a given requirement I Req_i associated to a resource R_k, the convenient pattern (Pat) is selected from the patterns set (Pats) thanks to the selection function (σ) that extract the pattern which name (PatN) matches the requirement type (RT) and which pattern goal (PatG) matches the resource goal(RG):

$$Pat = \sigma\,(Pats.PatN = \;Reqi.RT \; AND \; Pats.PatG \; = Reqi.RG)(Pats); \qquad (6)$$

The selected pattern is used to instantiate the corresponding policy rule. According to this, a policy rule refereeing to the requirement and the resource is generated. Let R_k be the resource associated to the ith requirement Reqi, (i.e. $R_k = Req_i.RR$), the policy rule which refers to this requirement and to the kth resource is defined as:

$$PolR_{ik} = (Req_i.RR, \; Pat.PatN, \; Pat.PatG, \; Req_i.RL, \; Req_i.RC, Pat) \qquad (7)$$

After generating the 'basic policy rule' thanks to this selection process, we have to check the selected pattern's related sub-pattern to get more precise policy rules. If a selected pattern contains a related sub-pattern (i.e. when Pat.PatR is not an empty set), a refinement algorithm is recursively launched to precise and develop the policy rules associated to this pattern (for example, a generic "confidentiality management" pattern can be refined using authentication and authorization patterns as well as encryption sub-patterns).

At the end of this step the different policy rules associated to the requirements are generated. As for the CIM elicitation, we use a policy composition process, including the functional composition knowledge, to select, extract and compose the different policy rules attached to a resource. Each task (in the BL level) is considered as a sub-process and used to compose/derive the policies associated to same or lower-level resources composed to implement this sub-process. To this end, we extract high-level resource's associated same or lower-level resources, then we propagate high-level resource's each policy rule to associated lower-level resources.

3.4   Key Performance Indicator Evolution and Lifecycle Management

In our governance solution, each Monitoring Policy Rule invokes associated a Key Performance Indicator to monitor performance level of the governed object. As a consequence, high level governance requirements can be refined to generate lots of Monitoring Policy Rules, and then lots of Key Performance Indicators need to be managed. Furthermore, due to the changing of business requirements and quality ranges, it requires to update Key Performance Indicator adjusting quality range and eliminating useless Key Performance Indicators.

To simplify Key Performance Indicator management and to allow Business Decision Makers to make decision efficiently without getting interference from massive useless information, we take advantage of genetic algorithm to design a Key Performance Indicator Evolution process. This process aims at eliminating useless Key Performance Indicators and reducing monitoring errors to allow governance management to focus on the most active Key Performance Indicators and getting accurate monitoring results. Respecting the biological immunity process, we divide a Key Performance Indicator's monitoring results into two types:

- A "self" result means it is a satisfied result according to governance agreement. A "distance" is defined to measure the difference between a monitoring result and the associated required result. If a "distance = D[0]" means this monitoring result matches the associated required result, this is a satisfied result (self).
- A "non-self" result means it is an unsatisfied result which should trigger an alert to arise the attention of Business Decision Makers. The "distance" between "non-self" and the associated required result is defined as "distance = D[1]".
- All monitoring performance results (AP) are composed by "self" and "non-self".

Due to the complexity of collaborative business context, too many False Positive Errors and False Negative Errors can make the monitoring meaningless. We define a False Positive Error as a Key Performance Indicator which alarms a satisfied result as an unsatisfied result. A False Negative Error is a Key Performance Indicator detects an unsatisfied result as a satisfied result. These errors usually occur when Business Decision Makers change their business requirements and re-define quality ranges. In a dynamic business context, it requires to avoid these monitoring errors. To address this problem and to achieve flexible and autonomic Key Performance Indicators management, we define the Key Performance Indicator's evolution process includes three strategies:

1. Define a four-stage Key Performance Indicator lifecycle,
2. Define a self-tolerance strategy,
3. Define a self-variation strategy.

The four-stage lifecycle aims at managing Key Performance Indicator Evoluation automatically and eliminating those which make enough False Positive/Negative Errors:

- (A) Immature KPI (I_{KPI}): initialized Key Performance Indicator which is invoked after required business scenario is built. I_{KPI} has to experience a self-tolerance period. It will be eliminated (go to Dead stage) if I_{KPI} alarmed self. If it survives from the self-tolerance period, it will evolve to mature Key Performance Indicator (T_{KPI}).
- (B) Mature KPI (T_{KPI}): Key Performance Indicator has passed self-tolerance which has a fixed mature lifetime. A Mature Key Performance Indicator detects and alarms enough "non-self" it can evolve to Memory stage. Otherwise, if it is too old or it alarms "self", it goes to Dead stage.

- (C) Memory KPI (M_{KPI}): Memory stage is a stable stage. Key Performance Indicator has detected enough unsatisfied results. A Memory Key Performance Indicator has unlimited lifetime, but once it alarms "self", it goes to Dead stage.
- (D) Dead KPI: Key Performance Indicator has alarmed self or it is too old. Dead KPI should be eliminated.

Viable Key Performance Indicators (V_{KPIs}) are composed by T_{KPI} and M_{KPI}:

$$V_{KPI} = T_{KPI} \cup M_{KPI}; \quad T_{KPI} \cap M_{KPI} = \phi; \tag{8}$$

Then, the Self-tolerance strategy aims at eliminating those Key Performance Indicators which made enough False Positive Errors. If a Key Performance Indicator alarms enough satisfied results as unsatisfied results, it goes to Dead stage which means it is eliminated. Then, the self variation strategy aims at adapting the definition of "self" (satisfied result) dynamically to fit the ever-changed business requirements.

Multi-cloud provides a dynamic environment. It is transforming the way computing resources are orchestrated. Definition of wastes and values should be adapted to fit this dynamic context and to satisfy users' ever-changed requirements. As a consequence, the definition of satisfied result should be dynamically adapted to fit business requirements, the set of "self" should be adapted accordingly. To this end we define self variation:

$$Self(t) = \begin{cases} \{x_1, x_2, \ldots, x_n\} & t = 0 \\ self(t-1) - self_{variation}(t) \cup self_{new}(t), & t \geq 0 \end{cases} \tag{9}$$

$$self_{variation} = \{x | x \in self(t-1), \exists y \in V_{KPI}(t-1) (f_{check}(y,x) = 2 \wedge f_{confirm}(x) = 0)\} \tag{10}$$

$Self_{variation}$ is the set of mutated self-elements representing current abnormal activities.

$Self_{new}(t) = \{y | y$ is the new self-element collected at time t$\}$

$Self_{new}(t)$ is the newly defined self-elements at time t.

$$f_{check}(y,x) = \begin{cases} 2 f_{m-list}(y.x) = 1 \wedge x \in & self(t-1) \\ 1 f_{m-list}(y,x) = 1 \wedge x \notin & self(t-1) \\ 0 & otherwise \end{cases} \tag{11}$$

$f_{check}(y, x)(y \in V_{KPI}, x \in AP)$ is used to classify monitored execution of policy rule either identified as self or non-self. If x is matched with new self and does not belong to self(t−1), then x is sure a non-self and 1 is returned. If x is matched with new self and belongs to self(t−1), then x may be a non-self (needs to be confirmed by administrator), and 2 is returned. If x is not matched with new self, then x is identified as a self, then 0 is returned.

$$f_{confirm}(x) = \begin{cases} 1 & x \text{ is a self confirmaed by administrator} \\ 0 & otherwise \end{cases} \qquad (12)$$

$$V_{KPI}(t) = M_{KPI}(t) \cup T_{KPI}(t) \; t \geq 0 \qquad (13)$$

This model is able to delete the mutated self (self$_{variation}$) in time through self-immune surveillance. Therefore, the false-negative error can be reduced. As this model can extend the depiction scope of self through adding new self (Self$_{new}$) into self-set. Therefore, the false-positive error can also be reduced.

This model simulates the lymphocytes growth in the marrow, an initial immature Key Performance Indicator needs to go through this self-tolerance process in a given time period evolve to a mature Key Performance Indicator.

$$I_{KPI} = \begin{cases} \{x_1, x_2, \ldots, x_\xi\} & t = 0 \\ I_{tolerance}(t) - I_{maturation}(t) \cup I_{new}(t) & t \geq 1 \end{cases} \qquad (14)$$

$$I_{tolerance}(t) = \{y | y.distance = x.distance, y.age = x.age + 1, x \in (t-1)$$
$$- \{X | X \in I_{KPI} \;\; (t-1), \exists y \in self(t-1)f(m-list)(x,y) = 1\}) \qquad (15)$$

$I_{tolerance}$ is the set of surviving I_{KPI} in $I_{KPI}(t-1)$ after one step of tolerance processes, I_{KPI} should go through α steps of tolerance processes and then evolve to T_{KPI}.

$$I_{maturatin} = (t) = \{X \in I_{tolerance}(t), x.age > \alpha\} \qquad (16)$$

$I_{maturation}$ have undergone α steps of tolerance processes at time t.

$$I_{new}(t) = \{y1, y2, \ldots, y\xi\} \qquad (17)$$

I_{new} is the set of new immature Key Performance Indicators generated randomly at time t.

Respecting the biological immune evolution process, we define Mature Key Performance Indicators (T_{KPIs}) associated to a fixed lifetime (λ). A Mature Key Performance Indicator (T_{KPI}) can evolve to a Memory Key Performance Indicator (M_{KPI}) when it detects enough non-self (count $\geq \beta$). Otherwise, if it cannot detect enough non-self or if it detects "self", it is replaced by newly generated T_{KPI}.

$$T_{KPI}(t) \begin{cases} \phi & t = 0 \\ T'_{KPI} \cup T_{new}(t) - T_{memory}(t) - T_{dead}(t) & t \geq 1 \end{cases} \qquad (18)$$

$T'_{KPI}(t)$: T_{KPI} undergoes one step of evolution, $T''_{KPI}(t)$: T_{KPI} is getting 2 steps older. T_{dead} is the set of Key Performance Indicators that haven't matched enough Non-self (count $\leq \beta$) in their lifetime(λ) or if they did false positive error at time t. T_{clone} the clone process of mature Key Performance Indicator.

During T_{KPI}'s lifetime, the inefficient Key Performance Indicator will be killed through the clone selection processes. Efficient Key Performance Indicators will evolve to M_{KPI}.

$ap_i \in AP$ (AP is the set of all monitoring performance results including self and non-self)

$$T''_{KPI} = \{y | y.ap = x.ap, y.age = x.age + 1, y.count = x.count, \in T_{KPI}(t - 1)\} \quad (19)$$

$$T_{clone}(t) = \{y\} y.ap = x.ap, \ y.age, \ y.count = x.count + 1, \ x.count \geq \beta\} \quad (20)$$

$$T_{new}(t) = \{y | y.ap = x.ap, \ y.age = 0, \ y.count = 0, \ x \in \text{Imaturation}(t)\} \quad (21)$$

$$T_{memory}(t) = \{x | x \in T'KPI(t), x.count \geq \beta\} \cup \{x | x \in T''_{KPI}(t) \wedge \exists y \in AP(t-1) f_{check}(x, y) = 2 \wedge f_{confirm}(y) = 1\} \quad (22)$$

T_{memory} is the set of newly generated memory Key Performance Indicators. A memory Key Performance Indicator will be deleted if it makes false-positive error which means a M_{KPI} alarms a normal activity. This dynamic model of immune memory, as well as other dynamic models discussed above can reduce both false positive error and false negative error and they can enhance the ability of self-adaptation for our governance execution system.

$$M_{KPI}(t) = \begin{cases} \phi & t = 0 \\ M_{KPI}(t-1) - M_{dead}(t) \cup T_{memory}(t) & t \geq 1 \end{cases} \quad (23)$$

3.5   Policy Model@Runtime

The policy rules (generated as XML files) are used to annotate each resource with the Non Functional Requirements. These policy rules are used at runtime to launch the monitoring/governance services. By this way KPI value can be acquired and/or computed. Then these monitoring KPI values are matched with the policy metric to check the compliance of the execution with the NFR (Non Functional Requirement). To achieve this process, monitoring/computing/governance services are composed and orchestrated "on the fly". This allows paying attention on precedence constraints between policy rules and contextual adaptation. For example, an authentication policy have to be applied before launching the authorization policy. In a similar way, the authorization policy must be applied to allow or deny the real service invocation. Then, to support the governance loop, after the execution KPIs results related to the resource are assembled according to the NFP groups in order to get the global view associated to each group of NFP.

4 Conclusions

To support governance functions and secured deployment in a multi-cloud context we proposed to take advantage of the MDE and pattern-based engineering approaches to generate NFP management policies depending on the deployment process. Our multi-level architecture built on the top of the XaaS model allows taking advantage of the Business knowledge to derive and compose policy rules at each layer based on a single business requirement and deploy them depending on the execution context. Further works will focus on the service orchestrator component so that the policy rules will be used to compose and orchestrate the NFP management and governance services "on the fly" depending on the exact deployment context.

Acknowledgements. This work has been partly supported by the French Economy Ministry DGCIS under the Web Innovant Process 2.0 project grant.

References

1. Gartner, Inc. analysts: Gartner Report. Top 10 Strategic Technologies for 2012 (2012)
2. DMTF Informational: Interoperable Clouds – A White Paper from the Open Cloud Standards Incubator (2009)
3. Mell, P., Grance, T.: The NIST Definition of Cloud Computing. NIST Special Publication 800–145 (2011)
4. Zhang, Q., Cheng, L., Boutaba, R.: Cloud computing: State-of-the-art and research challenges. J: Internet Serv. Appl. 1(1), 7–18 (2010)
5. Rodero-Merino, L., Vaquero, L.M., Gil, V., Galán, F., Fontán, J.J., Montero, R.S., Llorente, I.M.: From infrastructure delivery to service management in clouds. Future Gener. Comput. Syst. 26(8), 1226–1240 (2010)
6. Papazoglou, M., Van Den Heuvel, W.: Service-oriented design and development methodology. Int. J. Web Eng. Technol. 2(4), 412–442 (2006)
7. Freitas, A.L., Parlavantzas, N., Pazat, J.: An integrated approach for specifying and enforcing SLAs for cloud services. In: Proceedings of IEEE CLOUD, pp. 376–383 (2012)
8. Vaquero, L.M., Morán, D., Galán, F., Alcaraz-Calero, J.M.: Towards runtime reconfiguration of application control policies in the cloud. J. Netw. Syst. Manag. 20(4), 489–512 (2012)
9. Zhu, Q., Tung, T.: A performance interference model for managing consolidated workloads in QoS-aware clouds, cloud computing (CLOUD). In: 2012 IEEE 5th International Conference, pp. 170–179 (2012)
10. Jayasinghe, D., Swint, G., Malkowski, S., Li, J., Wang, Q, Park, J., Pu, C.: Expertus: a generator approach to automate performance testing in IaaS clouds. In: IEEE Fifth International Conference on Cloud Computing, pp. 115–122 (2012)
11. Moran, D., Vaquero, L.M., Galan, F.: Elastically ruling the cloud: specifying application's behavior in federated clouds. In: IEEE International Conference on Cloud Computing - CLOUD, pp. 89–96 (2011)

12. Clayman, S., Galis, A., Chapman, C., Toffetti, G., Rodero-Merino, L., Vaquero, L.M., Nagin, K., Rochwerger, B.: Monitoring service clouds in the future internet. In: Tselentis, G., Galis, A., Gavras, A., Krco, S., Lotz, V., Simperl, E., Stiller, B., Zahariadis, T. (eds.) Towards the Future Internet - Emerging Trends from European Research, pp. 115–126. IOS Press, Amsterdam (2010)
13. Garrison, G., Kim, S., Wakefield, R.L.: Success factors for deploying cloud computing. Commun. ACM **55**(9), 62–68 (2012)
14. Alhamad, M., Dillon, T., Chang, E.: A survey on SLA and performance measurement in cloud computing. In: Meersman, R., Dillon, T., Herrero, P., Kumar, A., Reichert, M., Qing, L., Ooi, B.-C., Damiani, E., Schmidt, D.C., White, J., Hauswirth, M., Hitzler, P., Mohania, M. (eds.) OTM 2011, Part II. LNCS, vol. 7045, pp. 469–477. Springer, Heidelberg (2011)
15. Katsaros, G., Kousiouris, G., Gogouvitis, S.V., Kyriazis, D., Menychtas, A., Varvarigou, T.: A Self-adaptive hierarchical monitoring mechanism for Clouds. J. Syst. Softw. **85**(5), 1029–1041 (2012)
16. Jureta, J.I., Herssens, C., Faulkner, S.: A comprehensive quality model for service-oriented systems. Softw. Q. Control **17**(1), 65–98 (2009)
17. Heward, G.: Assessing the performance impact of service monitoring. In: Proceedings of the 2010 21st Australian Software Engineering Conference (ASWEC '10). IEEE Computer Society, Washington, DC, USA (2010)
18. Gogouvitis, S., Konstanteli, K., Waldschmidt, S., Kousiouris, G., Katsaros, G., Menychtas, A., Kyriazis, D., Varvarigou, T.: Workflow management for soft real-time interactive applications in virtualized environments. Future Gener. Comput. Syst. **28**(1), 193–209 (2012)
19. Ouedraogo, W.F., Biennier, F., Ghodous, P.: Adaptive security policy model to deploy business process in cloud infrastructure. In: The 2nd International Conference on Cloud Computing and Services Science, CLOSER 2012. Porto, Portugal, pp. 287–290 (2012)
20. Cloud security alliance: Security Guidance for Critical Areas of Focus in Cloud Computing V3, (2012). https://cloudsecurityalliance.org/wp-content/themes/csa/guidance-download-box.php
21. Jericho Forum, Cloud Cube Model: Selecting Cloud Formations for Secure Collaboration, Jericho Forum, Version 1.0 (2009). http://www.opengroup.org/jericho/cloud_cube_model_v1.0.pdf
22. Marcos, E., Acuña, C.J., Cuesta, C.E.: Integrating Software Architecture into a MDA Framework. In: Gruhn, V., Oquendo, F. (eds.) EWSA 2006. LNCS, vol. 4344, pp. 127–143. Springer, Heidelberg (2006)
23. Van Der Straeten, R., Mens, T., Van Baelen, S.: Challenges in Model-Driven Software Engineering. In: Chaudron, M.R. (ed.) MODELS 2008. LNCS, vol. 5421, pp. 35–47. Springer, Heidelberg (2009)
24. Torres, V., Giner, P., Pelechano, V.: Developing BP-driven web applications through the use of MDE techniques. Softw. Syst. Model. **11**(4), 609–631 (2012)
25. Basin, D., Doser J., Lodderstedt, T.: Model driven security for process oriented systems. In: SACMAT '03: Proceedings of the Eighth ACM Symposium on Access Control Models and Technologies (2003)
26. Clavel, M., Silva, V., Braga, C., Egea, M.: Model-driven security in practice: an industrial experience. In: ECMDA-FA '08 Proceedings of the 4th European Conference on Model Driven Architecture: Foundations and Applications, pp. 326–337 (2008)

27. Souza, A.R., Silva, B.L., Lins, F.A., Damasceno, J.C., Rosa, N.S., Maciel, P.R., Medeiros, R.W., Stephenson, B., Motahari-Nezhad, H.R., Li, J., Northfleet, C.: Sec-MoSC Tooling - Incorporating Security Requirements into Service Composition. In: Baresi, L., Chi, C.-H., Suzuki, J. (eds.) ICSOC-ServiceWave 2009. LNCS, vol. 5900, pp. 649–650. Springer, Heidelberg (2009)

28. Wolter, C., Menzel, M., Schaad, A., Miseldine, P.: Model-driven business process security requirement specification. J. Syst. Archit. JSA **55**(4), 211–223 (2009)

29. Jürjens, J.: Model-based security engineering with UML. In: Aldini, A., Gorrieri, R., Martinelli, F. (eds.) FOSAD 2005. LNCS, vol. 3655, pp. 42–77. Springer, Heidelberg (2005)

30. Mülle, J., von Stackelberg, S., Böhm, K.: Security Language for BPMN Process Models. Karlsruhe institute of technology, Germany (2011)

31. Loganayagi, B., Sjuatha, S.: Enhance cloud security by combining virtualization and policy monitoring techniques. Procedia Eng. **30**, 654–661 (2012)

32. Li, J., Biennier, F., Amghar, Y.: Business as a Service governance in a Cloud organization. In: Proceedings of the I-ESA Conferences 6, Enterprise Interoperability V, pp. 355–365 (2012)

33. Yoshioka, N., Washizaki, H.: A survey on security patterns. Prog. Inform. **5**(5), 35–47 (2008)

34. Uzunov, A.V., Fernandez, E.B., Falkner, K.: Securing distributed systems using patterns: A survey. Comput. Secur. **31**(5), 681–703 (2012)

An Approach for Monitoring Components Generation and Deployment for SCA Applications

Mohamed Mohamed$^{(\boxtimes)}$, Djamel Belaïd, and Samir Tata

Institut MINES-TELECOM, TELECOM SudParis,
UMR CNRS Samovar, Evry, France
{mohamed.mohamed,djamel.belaid,samir.tata}@telecom-sudparis.eu

Abstract. Cloud Computing is an emerging paradigm involving different kind of Information Technologies (IT) services. One of the major advantages of this paradigm resides on its economic model based on *pay-as-you-go*. This paradigm got an increasing attention these last years regarding different aspects (e.g., deployment, scalability, elasticity), meanwhile, monitoring remains not well explored. Almost all the existing solutions for monitoring do not offer an approach that allows to describe in a granular way the monitoring requirements. Moreover, they do not take into account the scalability issues. In this paper, we propose a model that allows to describe monitoring requirements for Service Component Architecture (SCA) applications in different granularities. We propose an approach that transforms SCA components that were initially designed without monitoring facilities to render them monitorable. In our approach, we use a Micro-container based mechanism to deploy components in the Cloud. This mechanism ensures the scalability of SCA applications. Our solution take into account a late instantiation politic to reduce resources consumption to be in-line with the economic model of the Cloud. The realized experiments proves the efficiency of our solution.

Keywords: Cloud computing · Monitoring · SCA component model · Scalability · Service containers

1 Introduction

Over the last years, there has been an enormous shift in Information Technologies (IT) to Cloud Computing. Cloud Computing is a recent paradigm enabling an economic model for virtual resources provisioning. It refers to a model for enabling ubiquitous, convenient, on demand network access to a shared pool of configurable computing resources (e.g., networks, servers, storage, applications and services) that can be rapidly provisioned and released with minimal effort or service provider interaction [1]. In this paradigm, there are basically three layers

The work presented in this paper was partially funded by the French FUI CompatibeOne, the French FSN OpenPaaS and the European ITEA Easi-Clouds projects.

© Springer International Publishing Switzerland 2014
M. Helfert et al. (Eds.): CLOSER 2013, CCIS 453, pp. 86–102, 2014.
DOI: 10.1007/978-3-319-11561-0_6

of services known as "IaaS" for Infrastructure as a Service, "PaaS" for Platform as a Service and "SaaS" for Software as a Service.

As it is, the Cloud is well adapted to host Service-based applications that follow Service Oriented Architecture (SOA). SOA is a collection of services which communicate with each other. Such type of applications can be described using Service Component Architecture (SCA) as a composite description that contains a detailed description for different components of the application and links between them. All the elements in a composite must be described as one of the standard artifacts of the SCA meta-model. A well described composite can be transmitted to a SCA runtime (e.g. TUSCANY [2], Newton [3]) that instantiates the different components and links them as described in the composite, these aspects among others will be detailed in Sect. 2. In this paper we will focus in monitoring Component-based applications in the Cloud which remains a critical issue and should be done at the granularity of a component to keep its good QoS.

Monitoring process consists of informing the interested part (user or application component) about the changes of the monitored system properties or notifying it on a regular way or whenever a change has occurred. When applied on a Service Component Architecture in a Cloud environment, monitoring becomes a complicated problem that has to face many challenges: first, the description of the need to consume monitoring information must be explicitly described in different granularities independently of the type of the components (i.e., Network, Compute, Storage, Software, etc.). Moreover, the nature of monitored components and the way their status should be retrieved depends on the component being monitored which renders this task complicated. Finally, any monitoring solution must respect the scalability of the Cloud and should minimize the resources and energy consumption to be in-line with the economic model of this paradigm based on pay-as-you-go.

In this paper, we propose a framework that enables monitoring SCA-based applications in cloud environments and our contributions are: an extension for SCA meta-model to enable the description of a component's need to monitor properties of other components (Subsect. 3.1), a list of transformations that render a component monitorable even if it was designed without monitoring facilities showing how our framework transforms the extended-SCA description to a standard one (Subsect. 3.2), the integration of our monitoring solution with a scalable micro-container to respect the scalability of the cloud (Subsect. 3.3), and the implementation details and the primer experiments that prove the efficiency of our approach (Sect. 4).

Many attempts to provide monitoring applications in the Cloud exist in the state of the art detailed in Sect. 5, but as we will explain, almost all the proposed solutions give tooling solutions to monitor Cloud applications behavior. Furthermore, there is no approach that expects to monitor components that were not designed with monitoring facilities. In addition, almost all of the existing monitoring solutions either do not take care of scalability issue, or do not include an efficient solution to that problem. In our work, we propose a granular description of monitoring requirements, we are independent of the components types, we alleviate the developer task who can finally focus just in the business of his components and leave the non functional properties of monitoring to our framework and finally we reduce the memory consumption and we respect the scalability constraint by the use of the technique of micro-containers.

A previous version of our work was presented in [4]. In this new version, we use a generic example to show the efficiency of our proposal to reduce the components number used for monitoring. We updated the deployment mechanisms to avoid the redundant deployment of monitoring components. The modified architecture verifies if the generic components exists so it uses them, or else it generates and deploys new ones. Moreover, some components are temporarily disabled by our framework, they are enabled just when needed. This late instantiation politic reduces the memory and energy consumption.

2   Background

In this section, we will present the background of our work, in which we aim at adding the description of monitoring facilities to Service Component Architecture (SCA) [5]. We will start by defining SCA and its basic elements, then, we will define monitoring and its different models and related aspects.

2.1   Service Component Architecture

OASIS describes SCA [5] as a programming model for building applications and solutions based on a Service Oriented Architecture (SOA). One basic artifact of SCA is the component, which is the unit of construction for SCA. *"A component consists of a configured instance of a piece of code providing business functions. It offers its functions through service-oriented interfaces and may require functions offered by other components through service-oriented interfaces as well. SCA components can be implemented in Java, C++, and COBOL or as BPEL processes. Independent of whatever technology is used, every component relies on a common set of abstractions including services, references, properties and bindings"* [5]. A service describes what a component provides, i.e. its external interface. A reference specifies what a component needs from the other components or applications of the outside world. Services and references are matched and connected using wires or bindings. A component also defines one or more properties [5].

As defined by Szyperski [6] "A software component is a unit of decomposition with contractually specified interfaces and explicit context dependencies only". Thus, a component not only exposes its services but it also specifies its dependencies. Most of the existing component models [5, 7–9] allow specification of their dependencies for business services external to the component. However, they do not allow specification of their dependency for external properties. The ability to specify dependency for external properties has two important implications. First, it results in specification at relatively fine granularity thus helping the architects and designers in fine tuning the component's requirements. Second, this fine tuning helps in elaborating the contract between two components because the properties can be enriched with additional attributes that constrain the nature of the contract through appropriate policies. In a component-based application, monitoring must be defined at the granularity of a component to get a global view of the application.

In the next subsection, we introduce monitoring and its different aspects.

2.2   Monitoring

Monitoring consists of informing interested parts of the status of a property or a service. In our work, we consider two models of monitoring: monitoring by polling or by subscription. Polling is the simpler way of monitoring, as it allows the observer to request the current state of a property whenever there is a need. The interested component can generally interact with a specific interface that provides a getter of the needed property. Monitoring by subscription model is based on a publish/subscribe system which is defined as a set of nodes divided into publishers and subscribers. Subscribers express their interests by subscribing for specific notifications independently of the publishers. Publishers produce notifications that are asynchronously sent to subscribers whose subscriptions match these notifications [10]. Subscription allows an observing component to be notified about changes of monitored properties using one of the following modes: (1) The subscription on interval: it implies that the publisher (producer) broadcasts the state of its properties periodically to the subscribers (consumers); (2) The subscription on change: it implies that the publisher has to notify the subscribers whenever its properties changed. The monitoring by subscription on change mode contains various types of monitoring: (i) Property Changed Monitoring (PCM): the monitored component has to send notifications to all subscribers whenever a monitored property is changed, (ii) Method Call Monitoring (MCM): the monitored component sends notifications whenever one of the service's methods is invoked, and (iii) Execution Time Monitoring (ETM): the monitored component notifies the subscribers about the execution time whenever a service invocation occurred.

Our objective is to add monitoring aspects to SCA description and to use this latter to monitor deployed applications in the cloud.

3   Our Approach

To overtake the explained problems, we propose an extension to SCA meta-model to add monitoring capabilities to components.

3.1   Extended SCA Meta-Model

Since the existing SCA meta-model does not support the explicit description of Required Properties of a component, we decided to extend this meta-model

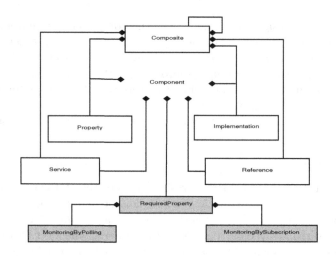

Fig. 1. Extended SCA with monitoring artifacts.

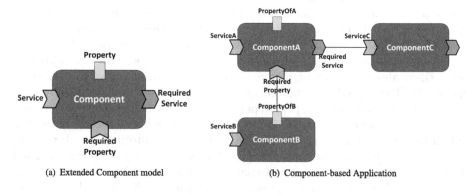

(a) Extended Component model   (b) Component-based Application

Fig. 2. Component-based application using required property.

by adding some artifacts allowing the description of monitoring capabilities for component-based applications. These new artifacts allow a component to express its need to monitor properties of other components with a specific monitoring model (i.e. by polling or by subscription) and with needed aspects related to monitoring. The newly added artifacts are the following:

- RequiredProperty: used to describe the need of a component to monitor one or more properties of another component;
- MonitoringByPolling: used to say that the required property is monitored using the monitoring by polling model;
- MonitoringBySubscription: used to say that the required property is monitored using the monitoring by subscription model.

The extended SCA meta-model is shown in Fig. 1. Some attributes related to monitoring may be declared for these artifacts like Start time of the subscription,

Duration of the subscription, Notification mode (on change or on interval), and Notification Interval if the Notification mode is on interval. The description of an application can be done using an Architecture Description Language (ADL). Instead of inventing a new ADL, we prefer to use one of the existing description languages. In this regard, SCA provides a rich ADL that details most of the aspects that we are looking for.

Figure 2(a) shows the main characteristics of the extended component. It provides a service through an interface and may require a service from other components through a reference. The component may expose properties through which it can be configured. In addition, it can specify its dependency on certain property. This required property, which appears at the bottom of the component, will be satisfied if we can link this component with another component that offers the requested property, thus, solving the dependency. Components can be combined together in a composite as an assembly of components to build complex applications as shown in Fig. 2(b). A component (A) can specify its need to monitor properties of another component (B) and use the service offered by the component (C). To explain our SCA extension, we take a generic example of a classic SCA-based application. The *ComponentA* is a component that requires to monitor the *propertyOfB* provided by *ComponentB*. This requirement is expressed using the *requiredProperty* element (Listing 1.1, Line 7). In this element, we can specify the monitoring type (i.e., by subscription or by polling), mode (i.e., on change or on interval) and scenario (i.e., using one channel or multi-channel).

Using the extended meta-model of SCA, we can describe an assembly application using our extended SCA ADL as shown in Listing 1.1.

Listing 1.1. Description of a SCA-based application using our extended SCA ADL.

```
1 <composite name="SampleApplicationomposite">
2  <service name="ServiceOfA" promote="ComponentA/ServiceOfA"
     />
3  <component name="ComponentA"  resource="pkg.ComponentA">
4   <service name="ServiceOfA" >
5    <interface.java interface="example.ServiceOfAInterface"/
       >
6   </service>
7   <requiredProperty resource="ComponentB.propertyOfB"
       monitoring="BySubscription" notificationMode="
       ON_CHANGE" multy_channel="true">
8    <property name="propertyOfB"/></requiredProperty>
9    ....
10  </component>
11  <component name="ComponentB"  resource="pkg.ComponentB">
12   <property name="propertyOfB">
13    <service name="serviceOfB" ><interface.javainterface="
       example.ServiceOfBInterface"/></service>
14    ....
15  </component>
16 </composite>
```

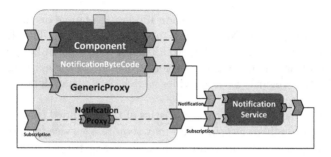

Fig. 3. Transformation for monitoring by subscription on change.

The extended SCA allows components to specify their needs to monitor other components' properties. However, these components can be designed without monitoring capabilities and cannot provide the status of their properties. To avoid this problem, our framework provides a list of transformations to apply to components to render them monitorable. In the next subsections, we introduce the main features of the monitoring mechanisms and their transformation processes.

GenericProxy Service. We have defined a general purpose interface GenericProxy that provides four generic methods. Each implementation of this interface is associated with a component for which the first method getProperties() returns the list of the properties of the component, the getPropertyValue() returns the value of a property, the setPropertyValue() changes the value of a property and the invoke() method invokes a given method on the associated component and returns the result. The transformations that render a component monitorable use a GenericProxy Component provided by our framework. It implements the GenericProxy Interface and the (proxy) services of that component. The byte-code of this implementation is generated dynamically by our framework.

3.2   Monitoring Transformations

Monitoring process consists in informing the interested component about the changes of required properties or notifying it on a regular way or for each variation. In [11] we have presented an approach for adding monitoring capabilities to components in the cloud in which we have considered two types of monitoring: monitoring by polling and monitoring by subscription. To complete the monitoring of any component from only the name and type of a property, the interested component often uses an appropriate interface that provides the method getPropertyValue(propertyName) to request the current state of a property.

If the component does not define its properties as monitorable, we need to transform it to make them to be monitorable, this can be done dynamically by our framework by adding to the byte code of the component an implementation of the predefined GenericProxy interface defined above and the needed byte code to send notifications (PCM, MCM or TEM).

The component can be then monitored by polling using the getProperty-Value() method provided by the newly added implementation. Our framework adds also a predefined component named *NotificationProxy* and a separate composite named *Notification Service*. *NotificationProxy* component plays an important role to reduce the number of loaded components at runtime. In fact, after the deployment of the transformed component, the *Notification Service* is not started in order to reduce the memory and energy consumption. The *NotificationProxy* is not linked to any *Notification Service* at the beginning. Whenever it receives a *subscribe* request, it instantiates the *Notification Service* that will handle the subscriptions and all the aspects related to notifications. It accepts clients subscriptions transferred by the *NotificationProxy*, receives notifications sent by the modified component and dispatches them to the interested subscribers. If the deployment scenario is one channel monitoring, all the newly generated composites will use one shared composite containing the *Notification Service*. However, if the scenario is multi-channel, each composite references an instance of the *Notification Service*. For this two cases, the *Notification Service* remains running whenever its subscribers list is not empty. If the list becomes empty, due to unsubscriptions or subscription expiry, this service is stopped to reduce the memory and energy consumption of the application. This strategy of reducing the consumption has no drawbacks on the monitoring latency time in our case because the *Notification Service* composite is a generic one and the needed time to start it is negligible. When the notification mode is on change for a required property of the monitored component, the *Notification Service* component offers a (callback) service of notification *Notification* to the modified component so that it can be notified of the changes of a required property and in turn inform all the subscribers of this change.

Transformation Example. Going back to the example previously described in Subsect. 3.1, we would like to transform the *ComponentB*, that it was designed without monitoring facilities, to render it monitorable by subscription on change. After applying the needed transformations on this component, we get a new composite offering the *ServiceOfB* and new monitoring services. The Fig. 3 describes the assembly after the transformations.

The newly created composite is described in the Listing 1.2. As shown in the figure, the transformation mechanisms transform the extended ADL description of the composite to a standard ADL description that could be instantiated using any SCA runtime.

Listing 1.2. Description of the monitored component after its transformation (one channel scenario) using SCA ADL.

```
1 <composite name="TransformedBComposite">
2  <service name="ServiceOfB" promote="ComponentB/ServiceOfB"
       />
3  <service name="GenericProxy" promote="ComponentB/
       GenericProxy" />
4  <service name="PCSubscriptionService" promote="
       MonitoringBySubscription/PCSubscriptionService" />
5  <reference name="notification" promote="ComponentB/
       notification"/>
6  <component name="ComponentB" resource="pkg.ComponentB">
7   <service name="ServiceOfB">
8    <interface.java interface="example.ServiceOfBeInterface"
        />
9   </service>
10   <implementation class="example.impl.
        ModifiedServiceOfBImpl"/>
11   <service name="GenericProxy">
12    <interface.java interface="GenericProxy"/>
13   </service>
14   <implementation  class="impl.GenericProxy"/>
15   <reference name="notification" target="
        OneChannelComposite/NotificationService"/>
16  </component>
17 </composite>
18 <composite name="OneChannelComposite">
19  <service name="NotificationService" promote="
        MonitoringBySubscription/NotificationService"/>
20  <service name="PCSubscriptionService" promote="
        MonitoringBySubscription/PCSubscriptionService"/>
21  <reference name="GenericProxy" promote="
        MonitoringBySubscription/GenericProxy" />
22  <component name="MonitoringBySubscription">
23   <service name="PCSubscriptionService">
24    <interface.java interface="
        PCSubscriptionServiceInterface" callback="
        NotificationServiceInterface"/>
25   </service>
26   <implementation  class="impl.MonitoringBySubscription"/>
27   <service name="NotificationService">
28    <interface.java interface="NotificationServiceInterface"
        />
29   </service>
30   <implementation  class="impl.Notification"/>
31   <reference name="GenericProxy" target="
        TransformedBComposite/GenericProxy"/>
32  </component>
33 </composite>
```

At this stage, we did not resolve yet the scalability issue related to the Cloud. To tackle this issue we use a framework based on scalable micro-containers technique. The next section describes this framework that we use to deploy components in the Cloud.

3.3   Deployment Within a Scalable Micro-Container

In [12], we introduced a new scalable and platform independent micro-container that enables components' deployment and execution in the Cloud. In this paper, we want to add monitoring capabilities to this micro-container. For optimality and performance constraints, features of the micro-container are as minimal as possible. The basic modules that make up the architecture of the Micro-container are those needed to ensure its minimal functionalities resumed at: (1) enabling the communication with clients, (2) query marshalling and demarshalling and (3) hosting a component and its context.

We designed a deployment framework able to generate this micro-container. This framework contains not only processing modules to ensure minimal micro-containers generation process, but also a set of generic elements for the submission and treatment of non-functional features to be included in the micro-container (HTTP, RMI or another generic communication, service administration tools, service billing, etc.).

To add monitoring capabilities to the micro-container, we use the component model that we presented in Subsect. 3.1 to represent components. Since some components can be designed without monitoring capabilities, we integrated the transformations presented in Subsect. 3.2 to render these components monitorable. And in order to integrate these transformations in our framework, we added the monitoring module to the deployment framework. This latter contains several modules shown in Fig. 4 and are as follows: (1) Processing Module: orchestrates all the steps to generate a micro-container, (2) Communication Generic Package: contains different packages implementing communication protocols, (3) Monitoring Module: supports different monitoring models, and (4) Assembly Module: generates a micro-container with monitoring capabilities.

To generate a micro-container with a composite hosted in, one must provide the needed implementations and the composite descriptor which describes how to assemble and deploy the micro-container into a Cloud environment. The processing module sends directly this descriptor to the assembly module before analyzing the implementation and generating the corresponding description. Then, the processing module detects the components' binding types and monitoring aspects. It selects the communication packages implementing the described bindings available at the Communication Generic Package and uses the chosen monitoring module to apply the needed transformations on the composite. Finally, it sends the new resulting implementation to the assembly module whose responsibility is to generate the new Micro-container enhanced with monitoring capabilities. Prior deploying the generated Micro-container, the *Deployment Framework* verifies if there is an already deployed Micro-container containing the *Notification Service* composite. If it is not the case, it generates a new Micro-container

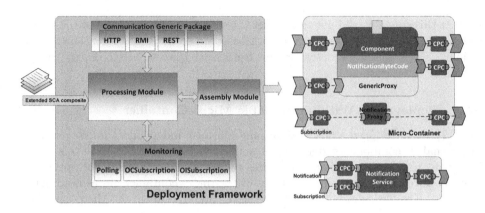

Fig. 4. Extension of the micro-container architecture with monitoring.

encapsulating the generic *Notification Service* composite. This is to assert that the generic *Notification Service* is deployed once and instantiated as much as needed.

As shown in Fig. 4, the Monitoring module supports monitoring by polling and monitoring by subscription with its two modes: on interval and on change. Monitoring on change mode includes Property Changed Monitoring, Method Call Monitoring and Time Execution Monitoring.

The generated micro-container (Fig. 4) is responsible of managing its communication with the clients, holding its service and processing all incoming or outgoing messages. These communication aspects are handled using a Communication and Processing Component (see CPC component in Fig. 4). Moreover, it is important to notice that the client can interact with the micro-container either to invoke the contained service, or to request monitoring information. It can also send subscription requests to receive notifications on change or on interval.

To prove the efficiency of our approach, in the next section, we describe the implementation of our scalable micro-container enhanced with monitoring.

4   Implementation and Experimentation

In order to test our work we implemented the previously described framework and we performed a list of experiments. In this section, we describe the implementation aspects and chain up by presenting the experiments results.

4.1   Implementation

The implementation process took place in different phases. We have first developed a minimal Java deployment framework, which allows developers to deploy a Java service on a hard-coded micro-container before deploying both of them in the cloud. To enhance the performance of the platform and facilitates updates and future changes, the deployment framework is made modular to allow us to plug or unplug modules. The generation process is based primarily on the parsing of the extended SCA composite.

The next phase was implementing a prototype of the monitoring framework as services that offer the transformation mechanisms to the components.

The byte-code of a *GenericProxy* component is generated dynamically. For this required byte-code level manipulation we used the Java reflection API and the open source software JAVA programming ASSISTant (Javassist) library [13]. The Java reflection API [14] provides classes and interfaces for obtaining reflective information about classes and objects. Reflection allows programmatic access to information about the fields, methods and constructors of loaded classes, and the use of reflected fields, methods, and constructors to operate on their underlying counterparts on objects. Javassist is a class library for editing Java byte-codes; it enables Java programs to define a new class and to modify a class file when the Java Virtual Machine (JVM) loads it.

The last phase was implementing a prototype of the monitoring framework as services that offer the transformation mechanisms to the applications. The byte-code of a *GenericProxy* component is generated dynamically. For this required byte-code level manipulation we used the Java reflection API and the open source software JAVA programming ASSISTant (Javassist) library [13]. The Java reflection API provides classes and interfaces for obtaining reflective information about classes and objects [14]. Reflection allows programmatic access to information about the fields, methods and constructors of loaded classes, and the use of reflected fields, methods, and constructors to operate on their underlying counterparts on objects. Javassist is a class library for editing Java byte-codes; it enables Java programs to define a new class and to modify a class file when the Java Virtual Machine (JVM) loads it.

The next subsection presents some experiments of our micro-container enhanced with monitoring capabilities, related to memory consumption and notifications' latency time.

4.2 Experimentation

In our work, we propose a platform able to deploy components in the Cloud on top of scalable micro-containers, with the capability of transforming components to be monitorable even if they were not designed with monitoring facilities. The proposed monitoring system is flexible in the way of choosing the best deployment scenario to meet the deployer requirements. As far as we know, almost all of the existing monitoring solutions use one channel to deliver monitoring information, but in our approach we exhibit the possibility of using a channel at the granularity of a component. In our experiments, we compare the results obtained using one channel for all publishers and using one channel per publisher. For our experiments, we have considered two criteria: (1) Memory consumption: Memory size consumed by the micro-container with or without monitoring facilities, and (2) Notification Latency Time: The elapsed time between the occurrence of the event and the notification reception from all subscribers. To perform these tests we used the NCF (Network and Cloud Federation) experimental platform deployed at Telecom SudParis France. The NCF experimental platform aims at merging networks and Cloud concepts, technologies and architectures into one common system. NCF users can acquire virtual resources to deploy and validate their own solutions and architectures. The hardware component of the network is in constant evolution and has for information: 380 Cores Intel Xeon Nehalem, 1.17 TB RAM and 100 TB as shared storage. Two Cloud managers allow managing this infrastructure and virtual resources i.e. OpenNebula [15] and OpenStack [16]. In our case, we used OpenNebula which is a virtual infrastructure engine that provides the needed functionality to deploy and manage virtual machines (VMs) on a pool of distributed physical resources. To create a VM, we can use one of the three predefined templates offered by OpenNebula i.e. SMALL, MEDIUM and LARGE, or we can specify a new template. During our experiments, we used our specific template with the following characteristics: 4 cores (2.66 GHZ each core) and 4 Gigabytes of RAM. To perform our tests, we defined two scenarios that reflect the objectives that we want to highlight in our experiments. The details of these experiments are: (1) Compare micro-container memory consumption before and after adding monitoring facilities to estimate the overhead of the monitoring module on the micro-container consumption, and (2) Compare notification latency time in the micro-container using monitoring system with one channel or monitoring system with multi-channels (i.e. one channel per micro-container).

In the different series of tests, we deployed different numbers of services on top of the micro-container. The used service in these experiments is a service that has a changing property. Whenever this property changes the service sends a notification to its channel (Notification Service component) which pushes this notification to all the subscribers.

In the first series we deployed services on micro-containers without monitoring capabilities and we took memory consumption measurements for each number. Then, we deployed the same number of services on top of the micro-container enhanced with the monitoring module. The purpose of this experiment was to estimate the overhead of the monitoring module on the memory consumption of the micro-container. Figure 5 shows the different values stored during these series including the JVM size.

These experiments show that the overhead of the monitoring module on the memory consumption of the micro-container is fair. In fact, the memory consumption is linear, increasing with the number of deployed services. The results show that the overhead of the memory consumption using one channel is more important than the overhead using multi-channel scenario. That can be explained by the fact of adding an extra JVM containing the channel and that adds the extra memory consumption noticed in the Fig. 5.

In the second series of tests, we aimed to compare the notification latency time using the micro-container enhanced with monitoring mechanisms in the two cases: using one channel and multi channel monitoring. Each series, we fixed the number of deployed services and we changed the frequency of events

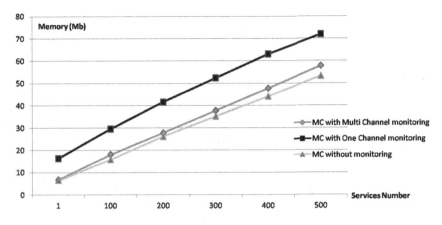

Fig. 5. Experimenting memory consumption of different types of micro-containers.

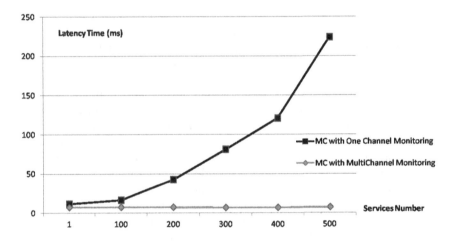

Fig. 6. Experimenting latency time using different scenarios of monitoring.

occurrence. After storing these measurements, we calculate the average latency time for each series. The stored values are shown in the Fig. 6. Specifically, these values represent the needed time from the event's raise till the reception of the notification by all subscribers. When the number of events becomes important, the channel is exposed to a big number of notifications, since all notifications are targeting the same channel. This latter should forward each notification to the list of the interested subscribers. When using a multi-channel system, every micro-container contains its own channel. Consequently, it is asked to manage just its own notifications. It will deal with a less number of notifications and subscribers. That explains the results shown in the Fig. 6 where the notifications' latency time is almost the same using the multi-channel monitoring system and it is increasing proportionally with the number of services when we use micro-containers with one channel monitoring system.

The next section exposes some approaches that tackled monitoring in cloud environments and ends with comparing these approaches against our approach.

5   Related Work

In the literature, there are many attempts to provide monitoring applications in the Cloud and in distributed systems. In this section, we present some proposed approaches in the monitoring area. We conclude by explaining the limitations of these approaches.

Nagios [17] is an open-source core system for network monitoring. It allows monitoring IT infrastructure to ensure that systems, applications and services are functioning properly. Monitoring can be applied on private or public services (private services are services and attributes of a server and public services are those available across network). To monitor any target, Nagios uses a list of plug-in that would be executed to poll the target status. Plug-ins acts as an abstraction layer between the monitoring daemon and the monitored targets. It enables remote command execution to know the status of the monitored target. There are several plug-ins for different protocols as SNMP, NRPE or SSH. Monitoring using Nagios can result in high load on the monitoring server if applied on a large number of targets.

Ganglia [18] is a monitoring system for high performance computing systems. It is based on a hierarchical design targeted at federations of clusters. It uses a multi-cast-based listen/publish protocol. Within each cluster, Ganglia uses heart beats messages on a well known multi-cast address as the basis of a membership protocol. Membership is maintained by using the reception of a heartbeat as a sign that a node is available. Each node monitors its local resources and sends multi-cast packets containing monitoring data on a well known multi-cast address. All nodes listen for monitoring packets on the agreed multi-cast address to collect and maintain monitoring data for all other nodes [18]. Aggregation of monitoring data is done by polling child nodes at periodic intervals. Ganglia Monitoring is implemented as a collection of threads, each assigned a specific task: (1) Collect and publish thread: collects local node information and publishes it on a well known multi-cast channel, (2) Listening threads: listen on the multi-cast channel for monitoring data from other nodes and updates monitoring data storage, and (3) XML export threads: accept and process client requests for monitoring data. Ganglia Monitoring system assumes the presence of a native multi-cast capability, an assumption that does not hold for the Internet.

H. Huang et al. [19] proposed an approach to monitor resources in the cloud using a hybrid model combining push and pull models. In these models, there are three basic components, the Producer, the Consumer and the Directory services. In the Push model, whenever the producer detects a change in a resource's status, it sends information to the consumer. Otherwise, in the Pull model, it's the consumer who asks the producer periodically about the resource's status. It is obvious that these two models have advantages and weakness. The authors propose a hybrid model that can switch to the best suited model according to the user requirements. The user can define his tolerance to the status inaccuracy between the producer and the consumer. Using this value, an algorithm can switch between pull and push models. In this approach the producer is in charge of subscriptions and sending notifications for all interested subscribers.

Almost all of these monitoring approaches do not offer a granular description of monitoring requirements. They do not tackle the case where components are not designed to be monitored. Moreover, in the stated works, the monitoring systems do not address scalability issues nor memory and energy consumption. In contrast, in our approach, we provide a model to describe the monitoring requirements with a tunable granularity. We also provided needed mechanisms to render components monitorable even if they were not designed with monitoring facilities. Finally, we proposed to use a scalable micro-container enhanced with monitoring facilities to reconcile monitoring and scalability issues. Our approach adds more deployment flexibility enabling one channel monitoring (i.e., one channel for all monitored components) and multi-channel monitoring (i.e., one channel per monitored component).

6   Conclusions and Future Work

Monitoring remains an important task to efficiently manage the cloud, but is still a challenge to find a monitoring solution to reconcile the granular description for monitoring requirements, the efficiency of the monitoring solution and its scalability as well as the memory and energy consumption. In this paper, we provided an extension for Service Component Architecture to allow components to describe their need to monitor other components properties with a tunable granularity. Moreover, we proposed a framework that provides the needed mechanisms to apply transformations on components to render them monitorable even if they were not designed with monitoring capabilities. Then, we proposed a platform that encapsulates the transformed components on top of scalable micro-containers and deploys them in the Cloud. Finally, to show the efficiency of our framework, we described its implementation and we performed different experiments. Our future work includes using monitoring information to apply adaptations or reconfigurations on components during runtime. We aim to render monitoring transformations feasible even at runtime and not only at deployment time as it is the case currently. The challenge is to be able to apply a live transformation of the component and to dynamically adapt its links with the outside during runtime.

References

1. NIST: Final Version of NIST Cloud Computing Definition Published (2011). http://www.nist.gov/itl/csd/cloud-102511.cfm
2. Laws, S., Combellack, M., Mahbod, H., Nash, S.: Tuscany SCA in Action. Manning Publications, Stamford (2011)
3. Dunne, R.: Introduction to the Newton Project Distributed OSGi & SCA (2008)

4. Mohamed, M., Belaïd, D., Tata, S.: Monitoring of SCA-based applications in the cloud. In: CLOSER, pp. 47–57 (2013)
5. Open SOA Collaboration: Service Component Architecture (SCA): SCA Assembly Model v1.00 specifications (2008). http://www.osoa.org/
6. Szyperski, C.: Component Software: Beyond Object-Oriented Programming, 2nd edn. Addison-Wesley/ACM Press, Reading (2002)
7. Becker, C., Handte, M., Schiele, G., Rothermel, K.: PCOM - a component system for pervasive computing. In: IEEE International Conference on Pervasive Computing and Communications, PERCOM '04 (2004)
8. Bruneton, E., Coupaye, T., Leclercq, M., Quéma, V., Stefani, J.B.: The FRACTAL component model and its support in Java: experiences with auto-adaptive and reconfigurable systems. Softw. Pract. Experience **36**, 1257–1284 (2006)
9. OSGI: Open Services Gateway Initiative (1999). http://www.osgi.org
10. Baldoni, R., Beraldi, R., Piergiovanni, S., Virgillito, A.: Measuring notification loss in publish/subscribe communication systems. In: IEEE Pacific Rim International Symposium on Dependable Computing (2004)
11. Mohamed, M., Belaïd, D., Tata, S.: Adding monitoring and reconfiguration facilities for service-based applications in the cloud. In: IEEE 27th International Conference on Advanced Information Networking and Applications (AINA) (2013)
12. Yangui, S., Mohamed, M., Tata, S., Moalla, S.: Scalable service containers. In: IEEE International Conference on Cloud Computing Technology and Science (2011)
13. Chiba, S.: JAVA programming Assistant (2010). http://www.csg.is.titech.ac.jp/~chiba/javassist
14. Java 2 Platform API Specification: (2010). http://download-llnw.oracle.com/javase/1.4.2/docs/api/java/lang/reflect/package-summary.html
15. OpenNebula: OpenNebula (2012). http://opennebula.org
16. Openstack: Openstack (2012). http://www.openstack.org
17. Nagios: Nagios Documentation (2010). http://www.nagios.org/documentation
18. Massie, M.L., Chun, B.N., Culler, D.E.: The ganglia distributed monitoring system: design, implementation, and experience. Parallel Comput. **30**, 817–840 (2004)
19. Huang, H., Wang, L.: P&P: a combined push-pull model for resource monitoring in cloud computing environment. In: IEEE International Conference on Cloud Computing (2010)

Locations for Performance Ensuring Admission Control in Load Balanced Multi-tenant Systems

Manuel Loesch[1][✉] and Rouven Krebs[2]

[1] FZI Research Center for Information Technology,
Haid-und-Neu-Str. 10-14, 76131 Karlsruhe, Germany
`loesch@fzi.de`
[2] SAP AG, Applied Research, Dietmar-Hopp-Allee 16, 69190 Walldorf, Germany
`rouven.krebs@sap.com`

Abstract. In the context of Software as a Service offerings, multi-tenant applications (MTAs) allow to increase the efficiency by sharing one application instance among several customers. Due to the tight coupling and sharing of resources on all layers up to the application layer, customers may influence each other with regards to the performance they observe. Existing research on performance isolation of MTAs focuses on methods and concrete algorithms. In this paper, we present concerns that are raised when serving a high amount of users in a load balancing cluster with multiple MTA instances. We identified potential positions in such an architecture where performance isolation can be enforced based on request admission control. Considering various approaches for request-to-instance allocation, our discussion shows that different positions come along with specific pros and cons that have influence on the ability to performance-isolate tenants.

Keywords: Performance · Isolation · Architecture · Multi-Tenancy · PaaS

1 Introduction

Cloud computing is a model that enables ubiquitous and convenient on-demand access to computing resources [1] via the Internet, offered by a central provider. Economies of scale reduce costs of such systems. In addition, sharing of resources increases the overall utilization rate and allows to distribute static overheads among all consumers.

The NIST defines three service models for cloud computing [2]. Infrastructure as a Service (IaaS) provides access to hardware resources, usually by levering virtualization. Platform as a Service (PaaS) provides a complete runtime environment for applications following a well-defined programming model. Software as a Service (SaaS) offers on-demand access to pre-installed applications used remotely.

© Springer International Publishing Switzerland 2014
M. Helfert et al. (Eds.): CLOSER 2013, CCIS 453, pp. 103–113, 2014.
DOI: 10.1007/978-3-319-11561-0_7

Multi-tenancy is used in SaaS offerings to share one application instance between different tenants, including all underneath layers, in order to leverage cost saving potentials the most. At this, a tenant is defined as a group of users sharing the same view on an application. A view includes the data they access, the configuration, the user management, particular functionality, and non-functional properties [3]. Typically, a tenant is one customer such as a company. This way, multi-tenancy is an approach to share an application instance between multiple tenants by providing every tenant a dedicated share of the instance which is isolated from other shares.

1.1   Challenges

Since MTAs share the hardware, operating system, middleware and application instance, this leads to potential performance influences of different tenants. For potential cloud customers, performance problems are a major obstacle [4,5]. Consequently, it is one of the primary goals of cloud service providers to isolate different customers as much as possible in terms of performance.

Performance isolation exists if for customers working within their quotas, the performance is not affected when aggressive customers exceed their quotas [6]. Relating this definition to Service Level Agreements (SLAs) means that a decreased performance for the customers working within their quotas is acceptable as long as their performance is within their SLA guarantees. Within this paper we assume SLAs where the quota is defined by the request rate and the guarantees by the response time.

In order to fully leverage benefits of multi-tenancy, the goal is to realize an efficient performance isolation which means that a tenant's performance should only be throttled when (1) its quota is exceeded, and (2) he is responsible for performance degradation of other tenants. If violating the quota were the only criteria, free resources would unnecessarily be wasted.

Since customers have a divergent willingness to pay for performance, SaaS providers are furthermore interested in product diversification and providing different Quality of Service (QoS) levels when sharing application instances. This is only possible when having a mechanism to isolate the performance.

On the IaaS layer mutual performance influences can be handled by virtualization. However, on the SaaS layer where different tenants share one single application instance, the layer discrepancy between the operating system that handles resource management and the application that serves multiple tenants makes performance isolation harder to achieve. Multi-tenant aware PaaS solutions handle issues related to multi-tenancy transparent for the application developer in order to increase the efficiency of the development process. However, nowaday's PaaS solutions do not address the introduced performance issues.

When solving the problem of mutual performance influences in practice, it has to be considered that multi-tenant aware applications have to be highly scalable since typical use cases aim at serving a very large customer base with a huge number of simultaneous connections. Hence, one single application instance running on a dedicated server may not be enough and it is likely that more processing power is needed than a single server can offer.

1.2 Contribution

The introduction of a load balancing cluster where a load balancer acts as single endpoint to the tenants and forwards incoming requests to one of several MTA instances, results in the need for an architectural discussion. In addition to the development of algorithms that ensure performance isolation, it is also necessary to provide solutions that show how they can be applied in real-world environments. Hence, this paper identifies two essential conceptual concerns for performance isolation in multi-tenant systems with regards to the request distribution in a load balancing cluster. We defined three positions in an architecture where performance isolation can be enforced based on admission control. The discussion of their pros and cons with respect to the elaborated concerns helps to apply existing solutions in real-world environments.

The remainder of the paper is structured as follows. The related work in chapter 2 presents an overview of existing isolation mechanism as well as the current architectural discussions, and we outline the missing points in the ongoing research. Chapter 3 introduces the conceptual concerns related to the distribution of request. Chapter 4 evaluates various positions to enforce performance isolation in a load balancing cluster and the last chapter concludes the paper.

2 Related Work

The related work is twofold. The first part focuses on concrete methods and algorithms to isolate tenants with regards to the performance they observe, and the second part discusses conceptual issues. We start with an overview of the first part of related work.

Li et al. [7] focus on predicting performance anomalies and identifying aggressive tenants in order to apply an adoption strategy to ensure isolation. The adoption strategy itself is not addressed in detail, but it reduces the influence of the aggressive tenant on the others.

Lin et al. [8] regulate response times in order to provide different QoS for different tenants. For achieving this, they make use of a regulator which is based on feedback control theory. The proposed regulator is composed of two controllers. The first uses the average response times to apply admission control and regulate the request rate per tenant, the second uses the difference in service levels between tenants to regulate resource allocation through different thread priorities.

Wang et al. [9] developed a tenant-based resource demand estimation technique using Kalman filters. By predicting the current resource usage of a tenant, they were able to control the admission of incoming requests. Based on resource-related quotas, they achieved performance isolation.

In [6] four static mechanisms to realize performance isolation between tenants were identified and evaluated. Three of them leverage admission control, and one of them uses thread pool management mechanisms.

All of the above approaches miss to discuss architectural issues that become relevant when they have to be implemented. Furthermore, no solution discusses scenarios where more than one instance of the application is running as a result of horizontal scaling. After this overview of concrete methods, subsequently the second part of related work is presented which addresses MTAs and isolation on a conceptual level.

Guo et al. [10] discuss multiple isolation aspects relevant for MTAs on a conceptual level. Concerning performance isolation they propose Resource Partitioning, Request-based Admission Control and Resource Reservation as mechanisms to overcome the existing challenges. However, the paper does not focus on situations with several application instances.

Koziolek [11] evaluated several existing MTAs and derived a common architectural style. This architectural style follows the web application pattern with an additional data storage for tenant-related meta data (e.g., customization) and a meta data manager. The latter uses the data stored in the meta data storage to adapt the application to the tenants' specific needs once a request arrives at the system. However, Koziolek's architectural style does not support performance isolation.

In [3] various architectural concerns such as isolation, persistence, or the distribution of users in a load balancing cluster are presented and defined. Furthermore, an overview of the mutual influences of them is presented. The paper defines aspects relevant for the following chapter. However, it does not discuss in detail the information that are needed to ensure performance isolation. Further, the position of a potential admission control in a load-balanced cluster is not addressed.

3   Approaches for Request-to-Instance Allocation

In this chapter two major conceptual concerns with impact on the request allocation in a load balancing cluster of multiple MTA instances are presented.

3.1   Tenant Affinity

The need to horizontally scale out by using multiple processing nodes (i.e. real servers or virtual machines) to run application instances of the same application leads to different ways to couple tenants and application instances. For this purpose, the term affinity is used. It describes how requests of a tenant are bound to an application instance. Various types of affinity might be introduced because of technical limitations, or to increase the performance since it is likely to increases the cache hit rate when the users of one tenant use the same instance. However, sharing a tenant's context among application instances that are running on different processing nodes requires a shared database, or the use of synchronization mechanisms. Since this might be inefficient, tenants may be bound to certain application instances only. In [3], four different ways are described of how such a coupling of tenants and application instances can be realized:

1. *Non-affine*: Requests from each tenant can be handled by any application instance.
2. *Server-affine*: All requests from one tenant must be handled by the same application instance.
3. *Cluster-affine*: Requests from one tenant can be served by a fixed subgroup of all application instances and one application instance is exactly part of one subgroup.
4. *Inter-cluster affine*: Same as cluster-affine, but one application instance can be part of several subgroups.

3.2 Session Stickiness

Independent of tenant affinity, requests can be stateful or stateless. Stateless requests can always be handled by each available application instance. However, maintaining a user's temporary state over various requests may be required, especially in enterprise applications. This is described by the term session. A session is a sequence of interaction between a tenant's user and an application in which information from previous requests are tracked. For load balancing reasons, it is beneficial when requests of one session can still be handled by different application instances depending on the processing nodes' load. Hence, when dealing with stateful requests, it can be distinguished between two kinds of sessions:

1. *Non-sticky sessions* are sessions where each single request of a tenant's user can be handled by all available (depending on the tenant affinity) application instances. Single requests are not stuck to a certain server.
2. *Sticky sessions* are sessions where the first request and following requests of a tenant's user within a session have to be handled by the same application instance.

When using non-sticky sessions, the session context must be shared among relevant application instances. This results in an additional overhead. Consequently, it might be beneficial to use sticky sessions to avoid sharing of session information.

4   Examination of Different Positions in a Load-Balancing Cluster

In this chapter two aspects of request admission based performance isolation in a load balancing cluster of multiple MTA instances are discussed. First, the information availability at different positions in the requests processing flow, and second, the consequences of tenant and session affinity.

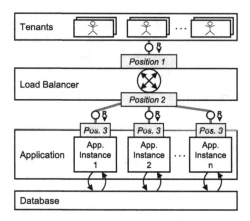

Fig. 1. Positions to enforce performance isolation.

4.1 Positions for Request Admission Control

An intermediary component such as a proxy will get different information at different positions in the process flow of a request. In Fig. 1, three possible positions to enforce performance isolation based on request admission control are depicted.

In front of the load balancer (Position 1) an intermediary has access to requests from all tenants, it can determine the response times and also whether a tenant is within its quota. The latter is relevant since performance isolation is based on the overall amount of requests from a tenant. However, it is not know which request is executed by which application instance since this is decided by the load balancer. The independence of the request distribution is a motivation for this position since it can allow for easier admission decisions. When fine-grained information about a processing nodes's internal state should be used by the isolation algorithm (e.g., resource utilization), access to this data is only possible with a notable communication overhead.

Directly after or included in the load balancer (Position 2), the information available is a superset of the information available at Position 1. In addition to the access to all requests and their response times, at this position, access to their distribution is given as well. It is known which application instance is responsible for which request and the overall amount of requests from each tenant is known as well. Again, the use of fine-grained information about a processing nodes's state comes along with a notable communication overhead.

In front of the application (Position 3) an intermediary has no information about other processing nodes, such as the number of requests they processed for a given tenant or their utilization. However, information about response times of the respective processing node are available. Compared to the other positions, fine-grained access to a processing node's internal state is possible with significantly less overhead since the component can be placed directly on the respective processing node. Further, no global knowledge about the other instances exists. If the information of all intermediaries is shared, this position would offer the same information as Position 2.

4.2   Comparison of Different Positions

In this section, the suitability of performance isolation at the three introduced positions is discussed with respect to tenant and session affinity. It is shown that the kind of tenant affinity and support of sticky sessions is a major decision for horizontal scalable MTAs. Besides load balancing, synchronization of data and support for session migration, it has big impact on performance isolation.

We assume that requests from each tenant are always homogeneously distributed over all available application instances if possible. Hence, accumulations of requests from a tenant to a single application instance are avoided and a clear separation of server-affinity and the other cases of affinity is given. From an information-centric point of view, it has to be noted that the required information for performance isolation and QoS differentiation is the same. Whenever it is possible to performance isolate tenants, it is also possible to give precedence to certain tenants by adding weighting factors when isolating them.

In Front of Load Balancer. *Server-affine.* In this scenario, performance isolation is not possible. An increase in response times and request rates can be measured. However, it can not be determined which request will be processed at which application instance since this information is maintained in the load balancer. Although it is known that requests from a tenant are always served by the same instance, the tenants that influence each other's performance by being bound to the same instance are not known. This makes it impossible to efficiently separate tenants. Sticky sessions have no influence on this since they do not provide information about which tenants are mutually influencing each other.

Non-affine. In this scenario, it depends on the session stickiness whether performance isolation is possible. Using non-sticky sessions, performance isolation is possible. In front of the load balancer it can be determined whether a tenant is within his quota since the full number of requests from a tenant is known. Furthermore, in case of non-sticky sessions, the load balancer can homogeneously distribute the requests. Hence, the more aggressive a tenant is, the more he is contributing to a bad performance of any tenant. With this knowledge, it is possible to performance-isolate tenants. However, when using sticky sessions, requests are bound to an unknown instance. In this case, interfering when one or more tenants experience a bad performance is not possible since requests are not uniformly distributed to the different instances, and hence not necessarily the most aggressive tenant is responsible for bad performances. While initial requests will be distributed homogeneously, it might end up with a significant number of sessions that spend more time than others. Thus, it is possible that the most aggressive tenant is bound to a processing node with no further load whereas a less aggressive tenant has to share a processing node's capacity and thus is responsible for the bad performance of other requests.

Cluster-affine. In this scenario, performance isolation is not possible. The behavior in terms of request allocation is the same as described in the non-affine case with sticky sessions: the underlying problem is that the request allocation information is missing and the uniform distribution of request workload can no longer be assumed since the available instances are limited to a subset which is not known at this position. This is not changed by sticky sessions since they only make existing request-to-instance allocations fix.

Directly After/Included in Load Balancer. At this position, performance isolation is possible in the server-affine, non-affine and cluster-affine scenario. The load balancer maintains state to enforce tenant affinity and the stickiness of sessions in order to allocate requests to instances. Hence, at this position the available information about tenant affinity and session stickiness is a superset of the information available at the two other positions. The information about the request allocation and the ability to measure response times allow to interfere and performance-isolate tenants. However, as already stated above, access to a processing nodes's state which may increase the quality of performance isolation is complicated and comes along with communication overhead.

In Front of Application. *Server-affine.* In this scenario, performance isolation is possible. Given server-affinity, requests are always processed by the same instance and hence, any information about other processing node does not come along with benefits. Since requests of a tenant are not spread over multiple instances, other processing nodes do not influence this tenant and it is possible to completely measure all information related to the specific tenant's performance. As requests are already bound to a specific instance, it is irrelevant whether sticky sessions are used or not.

Non-affine. In this scenario, performance isolation is not possible without further information. Since requests of tenants can be served by all instances, the load balancer is free to distribute the requests of all tenants. Hence, it can be assumed that requests of each tenant are homogeneously distributed over all instances. However, performance isolation is not possible as the information about the total number of request send by each tenant is not available. This way, it can not be determined whether a tenant's quota is exceeded. The use of sticky or non-sticky sessions does not change this since requests from a single tenant are still distributed over various instances. However, in the case of non-sticky sessions, performance isolation is possible when the processing capacity of the processing nodes is equal and the total number of instances is considered. Then, the overall request rate can be determined since a homogeneous distribution of the requests can be assumed. This makes it possible to determine whether a tenant's quota is exceeded. But in the case of sticky sessions, performance isolation is still not possible since a homogeneous distribution of requests cannot be assumed any more.

Table 1. Positions and feasibility of performance isolation.

Tenant Affinity	Session Stickiness	Pos. 1	Pos. 2	Pos. 3
affine	no	no	yes	yes
	yes	no	yes	yes
non	no	yes	yes	yes
	yes	no	yes	no
cluster	no	no	yes	yes
	yes	no	yes	no

Cluster-affine: In this scenario, it is not possible to realize performance isolation without further information. The behavior in terms of request allocation is the same as in the non-affine case with the limitation that the available set of instances is a smaller subset. Similar as in the former case, the problem is missing information about requests that are processed at other instances, which makes it impossible to determine quota violations. Again, there is no difference when non-sticky or sticky sessions are used since the latter only make the request-to-instance allocation fix. However, like in the non-affine case, performance isolation is possible in the case of non-sticky sessions when all processing nodes have the same processing capacity and the cluster size is known. Then, information can be projected from one processing node to another by assuming a homogeneous distribution of the load balancer. This allows to determine whether a tenant is within its quota and thus performance can be isolated since access to response times is given as well.

4.3   Summary and Implications

Table 1 summarizes the above discussion and shows the elaborated differences based on different kinds of tenant affinity and session stickiness. The stickiness of sessions is only influential in some cases. In the presence of a non- or cluster-affine behavior with session stickiness, a central management of request processing information with access to the allocation of requests to instances as well as the overall amount of requests is required in order to guarantee performance isolation. It was explained why, in many scenarios, performance isolation is not possible without information about the request distribution (Position 1), or directly in front of the application instance (Position 3). Offering a superset of the information available at the two other positions, Position 2 is the only one that allows to realize performance isolation for all affinity combinations.

5   Conclusions

It was shown that performance isolation between tenants is an important aspect in multi-tenant systems, and that serving a huge amount of tenants requires the existence of several application instances and a load balancer that distributes requests among them. While existing work focuses on concrete algorithms and techniques to enforce performance isolation, this paper focuses on a conceptual realization of performance isolation in a load-balanced multi-tenant system.

We were able to outline that, from an information-centric point of view, the best placement strategy for a performance isolation component that leverages request admission control is directly after the load balancing decision. At this position, information about the allocation of requests to processing nodes as well as the overall amount of requests from a tenant is given. It was shown that the positions before the load balancer, or directly before the applications have disadvantages which make it impossible to realize performance isolation in every scenario. However, the use of fine-grained information about a processing node's state may increase the quality of performance isolation and this is best possible when the component is placed at the respective processing node. Consequently, data has to be transmitted via the network in the other cases, which leads to a trade-off decision depending on the concrete scenario.

Our future research focuses on providing a complete architecture to enforce and evaluate performance isolation based on the here presented results.

References

1. Armbrust, M., Fox, A., Griffith, R., Joseph, A.D., Katz, R.H., Konwinski, A., Lee, G., Patterson, D.A., Rabkin, A., Stoica, I., Zaharia, M.: Above the clouds: a berkeley view of cloud computing. Technical report, EECS Department, University of California, Berkeley (2009)
2. Mell, P., Grance, T.: The NIST definition of cloud computing (Special Publication 800–145). Recommendations of the National Institute of Standards and Technology (2011)
3. Krebs, R., Momm, C., Kounev, S.: Architectural concerns in multi-tenant SaaS applications. In: Proceedings of the 2nd International Conference on Cloud Computing and Services Science (2012)
4. IBM: Dispelling the Vapor Around Cloud Computing. Whitepaper, IBM Corp. (2010)
5. Bitcurrent: Bitcurrent Cloud Computing Survey 2011. Technical report, Bitcurrent (2011)
6. Krebs, R., Momm, C., Kounev, S.: Metrics and techniques for quantifying performance isolation in cloud environments. In: Proceedings of the 8th ACM SIGSOFT International Conference on the Quality of Software Architectures (2012)
7. Li, X.H., Liu, T.C., Li, Y., Chen, Y.: SPIN: service performance isolation infrastructure in multi-tenancy environment. In: Bouguettaya, A., Krueger, I., Margaria, T. (eds.) ICSOC 2008. LNCS, vol. 5364, pp. 649–663. Springer, Heidelberg (2008)
8. Lin, H., Sun, K., Zhao, S., Han, Y.: Feedback-control-based performance regulation for multi-tenant applications. In: Proceedings of the 15th International Conference on Parallel and Distributed Systems (2009)
9. Wang, W., Huang, X., Qin, X., Zhang, W., Wei, J., Zhong, H.: Application-level CPU consumption estimation: towards performance isolation of multi-tenancy web applications. In: Proceedings of the 5th IEEE International Conference on Cloud Computing (2012)

10. Guo, C.J., Sun, W., Huang, Y., Wang, Z.H., Gao, B.: A framework for native multi-tenancy application development and management. In: Procceedings of the 4th IEEE International Conference on Enterprise Computing, E-Commerce, and E-Services (2007)
11. Koziolek, H.: The SPOSAD architectural style for multi-tenant software applications. In: Procceedings of the 9th Working IEEE/IFIP Conference on Software Architecture (2011)

A Study on Today's Cloud Environments for HPC Applications

Fan Ding[1(✉)], Dieter an Mey[2], Sandra Wienke[2], Ruisheng Zhang[3], and Lian Li[1]

[1] School of Mathematics and Statistics, Lanzhou University, Lanzhou, China
dingfan08@gmail.com, lil@lzu.edu.cn
[2] IT Center, RWTH Aachen University, Aachen, Germany
{anmey,wienke}@itc.rwth-aachen.de
[3] School of Information Science and Engineering, Lanzhou University, Lanzhou, China
zhangrs@lzu.edu.cn

Abstract. With the advance of information technology - as building smaller circuits and hardware with lower energy consumption - the power of HPC (High-Performance Computing) resources increases with the target to employ complex large-scaling applications. In traditional computing, an organization has to pay high costs to build an HPC platform by purchasing hardware and maintaining it afterwards. On-premises HPC resources may not satisfy the demand of scientific applications when more computing resources for large-scaling computations are requested than own resources are available. Especially for SMEs (small and medium-sized enterprises), a temporarily-increasing computing demand is challenging. Cloud computing, is an on-demand, pay-as-you-go model, that provides us with enormous, almost unlimited and scalable computing power in an instantly-available way. Therefore, it is a valuable topic to develop HPC applications for the cloud. In this paper, we focus on developing an HPC application deployment model based on the Windows Azure cloud platform, and an MPI framework for the execution of the application in the cloud. In addition, we present a combined HPC mode using cloud and on-premises resources together. Experiments that are employed on a Windows cluster and the Azure cloud are compared and their performance is analyzed with respect to the difference of the two platforms. Moreover, we study the applied scenarios for different HPC modes using cloud resources.

Keywords: Azure · Cloud · MPI · HPC · Azure HPC scheduler · SMEs

1 Introduction

High-performance computing (HPC) dedicates big processing power to compute-intensive complex applications for scientific research, engineering and academic subjects. From the mainframe era to clusters and then grid, more and more available computing resources can be employed by HPC applications on-premises. Nowadays we have come to the times of cloud computing. There are some differences to provide users with the resources between on-premises and cloud. On-premises require users to

© Springer International Publishing Switzerland 2014
M. Helfert et al. (Eds.): CLOSER 2013, CCIS 453, pp. 114–127, 2014.
DOI: 10.1007/978-3-319-11561-0_8

invest much cost in purchasing equipment and software for building their infrastructures at their initial development. This may be a challenge for some SMEs (small and medium-sized businesses) since they have not enough capability to invest. With cloud computing, users can obtain on-demand resources from cloud virtual servers not only for the basic infrastructure but also for the extra resources which can be used to process complex workloads that cannot be accomplished by the enterprise/researcher competence of its own. Moreover, the massive data centers in the cloud can meet the requirement of data-intensive applications. By means of these advantages of the cloud paradigm, it will be an inevitable trend to migrate the HPC applications into the cloud.

Nowadays, there are many cloud service platforms provided by different cloud vendors. The major cloud platforms include Amazon's Elastic Compute Cloud (EC2) [1], IBM SmartCloud [2], Google Apps [3] and Microsoft's Azure cloud [4]. Users can choose the different kind of cloud platform according to which level of cloud service they need. Generally, they provide three types of cloud services, SaaS (Software as a Service), PaaS (Platform as a Service) and IaaS (Infrastructure as a Service), also called service models. These platforms with their support for HPC have been summarized in Table 1. Many companies also provide HPC cloud services or cloud-like HPC resources. Penguin Computing on Demand (POD) [12] is a remote HPC services developed by Penguin in which users can employ HPC resources by pay-as-you-go. Sabalcore offers an HPC Cloud Service [13], which enables HPC systems to be available over internet on-demand. UNIVA has developed its cloud product UniCloud [14], which is a software as a cloud middleware, allowing any cloud resource to be utilized and extends cloud systems to the HPC user community - Grid Engine software - to build an HPC Cloud. R-HPC [15] offers the R-Cloud to provide users with HPC services billed by a per job basis. Cyclone [16] is SGI's cloud computing service which focuses on technical applications and offers HPC hardware in a non-virtualized environment.

Table 1. Major current cloud platforms.

Service vendor	Cloud platform	Description	Support for HPC
Amazon	EC2 (IaaS)	Provides scalable web services, enables users to change capacity quickly	Cluster Compute and Cluster GPU Instances
IBM	IBM SmartCloud (IaaS)	Allows users to operate and manage virtual machines and data storage according to their need	IBM HPC clouds
Microsoft	Windows Azure (PaaS)	Composed of Windows Azure, SQL Azure and Azure AppFabric	Azure HPC Scheduler
Google	Google Apps (SaaS)	Provisions web-based applications (Gmail, Google Talk and Google Calendar) and file storage (Google Docs)	Google Compute Engine [11]

From the point of view of a user, who is not familiar with complex computer configuration, it is difficult to migrate existing on-premises applications into the cloud because of the differences and the complex configuration of the user interface in these cloud platforms. Some methods or middleware which enable users to use cloud platforms easily are required by scientists and other potential users of cloud resources. Much work has been done to study how to take an existing application into the cloud. The work presented in paper [5] is similar to ours, but the authors focused on moving a web application to Azure. CloudSNAP also was a web deployment platform to deploy Java EE web applications into a Cloud infrastructure [6]. In paper [7], the authors developed a framework to execute an e-Science application on Azure platform through expending COMPSs programming framework. But all of these aforementioned efforts did not consider parallel computing for the compute-intensive applications in HPC.

In our paper, we take the advantage of Azure to develop a cloud deployment model through expending the Azure HPC scheduler [8]. Windows Azure is an open cloud platform developed by Microsoft on which users can build, deploy and manage applications across a global network of the Microsoft data center. Our work is based on the project 'Technical Cloud Computing for SMEs in Manufacturing'. In this project, the application "ZaKo3D" [9] developed by WZL (the Institute for Machine Tools and Production Engineering, RWTH Aachen University) [10], which aims to do FE-based (Finite Element) 3D Tooth Contact Analysis, is a high-performance technical computing software tool based on simulation of the tooth contact. It reads several geometry data of the flank and a FE-Model of a gear section as the software's variation and then performs a set of complex variation computations. As a result of the variation computations, one gets contact distance, loads and deflections on the tooth. Such a variation computation includes e.g. thousands of variants to be processed which lead to computing times of around months on a single desktop PC. Currently, this challenge is addressed by employing on-premises HPC resources which are available at RWTH Aachen University, e.g. if one variant takes 1 h computing time, the entire variant time for 5000 variations would take 5000 h computing time. This exceeds by far the capabilities even of multi-socket multi-core workstations are used, but can be well performed in parallel by an HPC cluster. But the small and medium-sized businesses in general can neither access those, nor do they maintain similar capabilities themselves. The availability of HPC resources in the cloud with a pay-on-demand model may significantly change this picture.

We also developed a case which deploys the "ZaKo3D" application on Azure according to our deployment model. This use case convinces SMEs to adopt cloud computing to address this computational challenge. Moreover, the original application is a serial version, as outlined before, to execute a large scale of variation calculation for a long time. It is a challenge for us to design an optimal method to improve the computing efficiency. We have established a framework to deploy the application on Azure which parallelizes the variation computation and run the application on Azure by using our deployment model. Moreover, we study a combined HPC mode by means of on-premises and cloud resources. In the combined mode, one HPC application can be executed on two kinds of platform resources simultaneously, considering each HPC platform has its advantage.

The rest of the paper is structured as follows. Section 2 introduce traditional HPC mode using on-premises resources. In Sect. 3, we introduce the Azure cloud and its module Azure HPC Scheduler. Section 4 describes our problem statement. Followed by our deployment model and framework for parallel execution of the Zako3D application on Azure presented in Sect. 5. In Sect. 6, we present a combined HPC mode using cloud and on-premises resources. In Sect. 7, we compare the runtime between on-premises and cloud for HPC by deploying our application on the RWTH Cluster and Azure. Moreover, we analyze the applied scenarios of different HPC modes by means of cloud computing. This analysis can be used as a reference point for potential users to consider whether employ the on-demand resources. Finally, Sect. 8 concludes the paper with a summary and future work.

2   HPC in Cluster

Comparing with common scientific computing, an application in HPC requires some special operation to ensure efficiency. The computing in HPC usually divides an HPC job into some small parts and distributes them on multiple machines (usually homogeneous) to perform them simultaneously. Traditional cluster HPC adopts some HPC management tools to scheduler job on computing resources, such as Torque or the Microsoft Windows HPC Job Scheduler. As described in Fig. 1, users submit their job from the HPC job scheduler of a head node and the job will be divided into some small parts with application logic according a rule specified by developer, and then distributes these application logics on computing nodes running Windows natively or to a virtual machine. Computing nodes could perform same application logics with different data or different application logics.

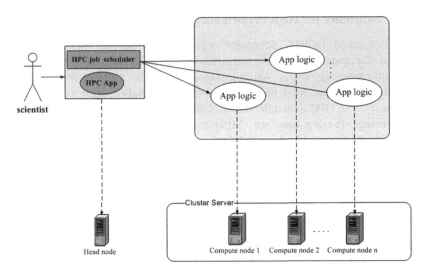

Fig. 1. The head node schedules an HPC job and distributes the application logics to computing nodes in the cluster.

3   Windows Azure and HPC Scheduler

In this section we introduce the Azure cloud platform and related technologies that we have used in the development of the deployment model architecture. The Windows Azure platform was announced by our collaborative partner Microsoft in 2010. In our work, they provided us the Azure cloud accounts for initial development and testing. This platform includes Windows Azure, SQL Azure and AppFabric. Our work focuses on Windows Azure, which is a Platform as a Service offering and provides us the compute resources and scalable storage services. We employ Windows Azure HPC Scheduler to deploy the serial ZaKo3D by means of an MPI-based framework developed by us, to the Azure compute resources. For data management, the Azure storage blob service facilitates the transfer and storage of massive data in the execution of our MPI application on the Azure cloud.

3.1   The Three Roles of Windows Azure

Windows Azure provides the user with three types of roles to develop a cloud application: Web Roles, Work Roles and VM Roles. Web Roles aim to display websites and present web applications, supported by IIS. Work Roles are used to execute tasks which require the compute resources. Work roles can communicate with other roles by means of Message queues as a choice in various techniques. The VM Role differs from the other two roles in that it acts as an IaaS to provide services instead of PaaS. The VM Role allows us to run a customized instance of Windows Server 2008 R2 in Windows Azure. It facilities migrate with some application, which is difficult to bring to cloud, into the cloud.

3.2   HPC Scheduler for High-Performance Computing in Azure Cloud

Microsoft developed the HPC Scheduler to support running HPC applications in the Azure cloud. Compute resources are virtualized as instances on Windows Azure. When an HPC application requires an Azure instance to execute, it means the work will be divided into lots of small work items, all running in parallel on many virtual machines simultaneously. The HPC Scheduler allows scheduling this kind of applications built to use the Message Passing Interface (MPI) and distributes their works across some instances. The deployment build with Windows Azure SDK includes a job scheduling module and a web portal to submit job and resource management.

The role types and the service topology can be defined when creating a service model in configuring cloud hosted service. HPC Scheduler supports Windows Azure roles through offering plug-ins. There are three types of nodes which provide different function and runtime support.

- Head Node: Windows Azure work role with HpcHeadNode plug-in, provides job scheduling and resource management functionality.
- Compute Node: Windows Azure work role with HpcComputeNode plug-in, provides runtime support for MPI and SOA.

- Front Node: Windows Azure web role with HpcFrontEnd plug-in, provides web portal (based on REST) as the job submission interface for HPC Scheduler.

Visual studio has been specified as the development environment for this component.

3.3   Azure Storage Blob Service

Azure storage service provides data storage and transfer to applications in Windows Azure and supports multiple types of data: binary, text data, message and structured data. It includes three types of storage service:

- Blobs (Binary Large Objects), the simplest way for storing binary and text data (up to 1 TB for each file) that can be accessed from anywhere in the world via HTTP or HTTPS.
- Tables, for storing non-relational data using structured storage method.
- Queues, for storing messages that may be accessed by a client, and communicate messages between two roles asynchronously.

In our deployment model, we employ the Blob storage service to manage our application's data because ZaKo3D uses text data for input files and output files. As described in Fig. 2, there are three layers in the concept of Blob storage. In order to store data into the Windows Azure with the blob storage service, a blob storage account has to be created which can contain multiple containers. A container looks like a folder in which we place our blob items.

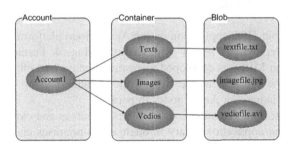

Fig. 2. Three layers concept of Blobs storage.

4   Problem Statement

As described in the introduction, ZaKo3D is a software package, part of the WZL Gear toolbox, and has been used to process the FE-based 3D Tooth Contact Analysis. It reads several geometric data of the flank and a FE-Model of a gear section as the software's variation. The results of the execution are the contact distance, loads and deflections on the tooth.

The variant computing will process a large numbers of variants. For example, there are 8 deviations at pinion and gear in the input data of one analysis, and each deviation with 4 values, so the number of variants the ZaKo3D needs to process is, $4^8 = 65536$ variants. Calculating such large amounts of variants one by one on a single PC, it would take way too long. Obviously, this traditional way does not work well. Our method is to split these variants and then compute them on different work units in the cloud in parallel. Figure 3 represents the variants description in the parameter input file. We consider ZaKo3D as an HPC application and develop an automatic parallel framework to distribute the parameter file over a fixed number of cloud nodes and execute the application in parallel.

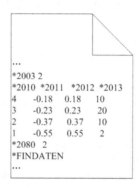

Fig. 3. ZaKo3D variation file.

5   HPC Application Deployment Model and Parallel Framework in Cloud

In order to deploy our HPC application on the Azure cloud platform, we developed an HPC application deployment model as described in Fig. 4. Furthermore, a parallel framework based on MPI was developed to ensure effective and efficient execution of the application. The function of the framework includes parsing variation file and distributing the variations on Azure nodes in parallel.

The deployment model combines on-premises resources and cloud resources. The scientist deploys the application binary through an on-premises cluster server or any windows desktop based on HPC Scheduler. All computing tasks will be processed by the Azure cloud computing resources.

5.1   Move Application to Cloud

Firstly, the head node and compute nodes on Azure have to be configured with Azure HPC Scheduler. The number of compute nodes as worker role in Azure is allowed to be set from the deployment interface according to the user's requirement. Secondly, after configuration for the cloud hosted service, there are two methods to move an application onto the configured Azure instance: from a local server and from a head node on the Azure portal. We focus on the way of using the head node. Here we have three steps: 1. Move the HPC application pack on the head node. 2. Upload the app package

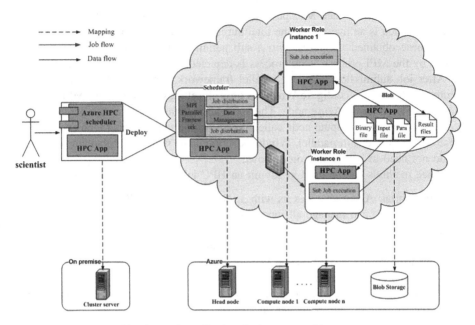

Fig. 4. HPC application deployment architecture.

to Azure blob storage. 3. Synchronize all compute nodes with the app package. These operations result in each compute instance maintaining a copy of the HPC application.

5.2   Parallel Framework and HPC Job Scheduler

As described in Fig. 4, the deployment module takes the application binary to Azure with a parallel framework based on MPI as the job scheduler. This framework aims to distribute and run in parallel the application binary onto Azure nodes. We take the ZaKo3D for example of HPC application. ZaKo3D is a serial application. It will take a long time for executing a number of parameters due to a large number of variation computations involved. Look back to the problem statement, the variation file needs to be divided and distributed to Azure nodes. When an HPC job in the cloud is scheduled, firstly, the framework will perform a distribution workflow for parsing the variation file and distributing variations (see Fig. 5), In order to ensure each node gets the same number of variations, the variation distribution workflow adopts loop method to distribute the variations to Azure nodes based MPI. After completing the variation

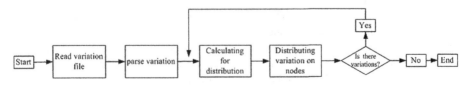

Fig. 5. Variation distribution workflow.

distribution workflow, each MPI process will get a part of the needed variation computations which is an average of the total number of variation computations, and then merge these obtained variations into a sub parameter file on different Azure nodes owned by the MPI process. This process is depicted by the job flow in Fig. 4.

After job submission with our parallel framework, the MPI job will execute on Azure which needs to configure Windows firewall settings to allow these MPI sub jobs to communicate across Azure node. The application binary with the sub parameter file is deployed on each compute node called Azure worker instance, and then executed on these allocated nodes in parallel. Windows Azure deals with load balancing for us, so we do not need to handle this on our own.

Three methods can be used to submit an HPC job by means of this model.

1. Azure portal: Azure provides us with a job portal in the HPC scheduler. Through this portal, we can manage all jobs, submit a new job or delete a job, or view the status of a job.
2. Command prompt on Azure node: job submission API is supported by Azure job submission interface similar as in Windows HPC Server 2008 R2 through a remote connection on the command prompt of an Azure node.
3. HpcJobManager on Azure node: an interface for submitting and monitoring jobs, similar to the HPC Job Manager on cluster.

5.3 Data Management

The data management in the framework, described by data flow in Fig. 4, is supported by a sub module which is dedicated to manage the application data on Blob storage, and gather output results from each compute node. The application data, which includes input files, library files and the application executable file, is synchronized on each compute node. As a result, all compute instances get a copy of the application. For gathering the work result, the results generated on each compute node are merged and then copied to the Blob Container by this module. Afterwards, results can be viewed and downloaded from the Azure web portal.

6   HPC in Combined Modes with Cloud and Cluster

As described in Sect. 5, we developed a deployment method that enables HPC application computing in parallel on a cloud platform. In real world, the advantage of cloud computing does not mean that HPC users intend to take existing applications entirely into cloud environment since clusters dominate HPC currently. Therefore, we present a combined mode which employs two kinds of resources.

Traditional HPC cluster have more power computing capability than cloud, but cloud can provide users on-demand resources and unlimited scalable resources. We can combine the two resources by means of their advantage to run HPC application.

As described in Fig. 6, the job submission in a combined mode is the same as in the traditional way, and the head node is hosted by one on-premises resource. The HPC job scheduler splits the application logics and distributes them on available computing resources for execution. The resources include local nodes and cloud nodes running on a cloud data center.

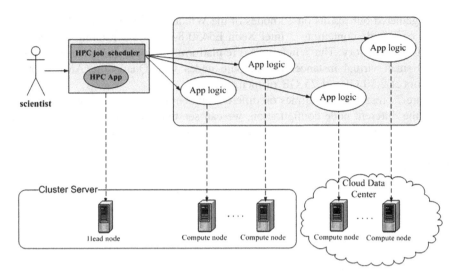

Fig. 6. HPC in combined mode.

Different from computing tasks running entirely in cluster or clouds, using this combined mode, extra work should be conducted by the HPC scheduler. Usually, the cloud nodes are not created on demand when a job is submitted, administrators have to work on the configuration of cloud nodes. The scheduler will also not automatically allocate any kind of resources to a job. Distributing application logics is according to the user's requirements: The user needs to specify which computing resources a task could employ, and whether the node is a cluster node or a cloud node.

7   Performance Analysis

7.1   Experiments and Performance Analysis

After running ZaKo3D on the Azure cloud, in order to compare the difference in performance between cloud and on-premises resource, we evaluate whether SMEs can profit from cloud's advantage in HPC. For that, we conduct a set of experiments on both Azure platform and the Compute Cluster of RWTH Aachen University.

We deployed ZaKo3D application with the developed parallel framework using our developed deployment model with the same number of variations (120) on the two different platforms. We distribute the work on respectively 1, 2, 3, 4, 5, 6, 8, 10, 12, 15 compute nodes of Azure and cluster (the number of instances to distribute variations must be the divisor of the number of variations depend on ZaKo3D), it means each experiment contains a job running on a different numbers of processors. It should be pointed out that there are some differences regarding the deployment on these two platforms: after the deployment of the application, all Azure nodes have a copy of the application data automatically, but using the cluster, we need to create a copy of the application data manually for each compute node.

We gathered our results on 15 nodes of the Windows part of the RWTH Compute Cluster, each node containing 2 Intel Xeon E5450 8-core CPU running at 3.00 GHz and 16 GB of memory. The Windows Azure platform can supply a hosted service with max 20 small virtual instances as compute nodes with Quad-Core AMD Opteron Processors at 2.10 GHz, 1.75 GB of memory.

Figure 7 presents the runtimes on different number of nodes of Cluster and Azure. Due to the different node configuration, we can see that the Azure's curve is always above the cluster one in low number of nodes. Azure's performance cannot catch up with the cluster. But as the number of compute nodes increases, the two curves will probably get close as depicted with 15 nodes in Fig. 7.

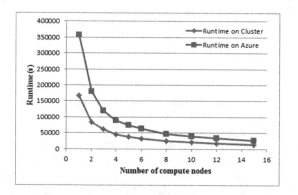

Fig. 7. Runtime of ZaKo3D on Cluster and Azure nodes.

We have also predicted the execution of application on high number of nodes in Cluster and Azure. We model an approximation of the runtime curve based on Amdahl's law.

$$t(n) = t_s + t_p(1)/n$$

In the formula, n equals the number of nodes, t(n) is runtime on n nodes. t_s is the runtime of the serial portion in ZaKo3D application and $t_p(1)$ the runtime of the parallelizable portion for n = 1. We get The best fit value for t_s and $t_p(1)$ by least squares from the measurements in Fig. 7.

$$Cluster: t_p(1) \approx 166217(s) t_s \approx 5579(s)$$
$$Cloud: t_p(1) \approx 353206(s) t_s \approx 3299(s)$$

Therefore, we can extrapolate the runtime on higher numbers of nodes, such as 100 nodes to 7241.17(s). As depicted in Fig. 8. We can see that there is a cross at about nodes 80, after this point, the runtime curve of Azure will be lower than cluster. It shows that the execution for HPC application in Azure can obtain better performance than Cluster in the high number of nodes.

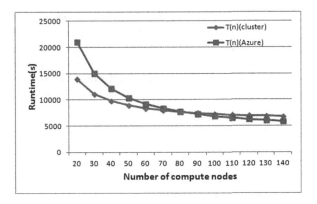

Fig. 8. Prediction of runtime by Amdahl's law on high number of nodes on Cluster and Azure.

Furthermore, from Fig. 9, we can see that scaling is well for a small number of nodes. However, due to the design of the application with a portion of 1.6 % sequential code, we are restricted by Amdahl's law and could get a maximum speedup of 58. We assume that applications with a higher portion of parallel code may scale well on Azure nodes for a high number of nodes. This indicates that cloud has good scalability and cloud's power can support HPC application's execution.

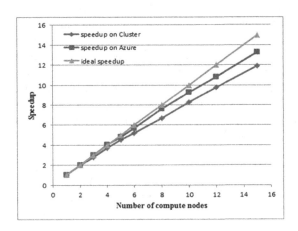

Fig. 9. Scalability of ZaKo3D execution on different number of Cluster and Azure nodes.

7.2   Applied Scenarios of Different HPC Modes in Cloud

The experiments demonstrate that cloud and cluster, each has advantages and disadvantages. Thereby, different scenarios can be used in different HPC modes in cloud.

- We can adopt the mode that computes tasks entirely using cloud resources in bellowed circumstances.

1. In the case that user's inadequate on-premises resources may not satisfy the requirements of large-scaling compute-intensive applications. Usually, the cheaper and on-demand cloud resources can meet HPC based on low costs.
2. On-premises HPC resources are in low utilization, such as a cluster is used only once time per month. It can not only increase utilization of paid resources, but also can obtain more economic benefit to take HPC tasks into cloud.

- To the combined modes from cloud and cluster, we can consider these circumstances

1. In an enterprise or organization, if their own computing resources cannot meet the requirements of HPC applications, they can employ extra resources from cloud platform to extend the scale of resources.
2. In the case that an enterprise or organization requires HPC resources temporarily. In HPC, it may happen that users need temporarily more resources to run their compute-intensive programs. If the organization buys a huge amount of hardware to be prepared for the peak of computing, a lot of resources will be unused in non-peak periods. If cluster resources are combined with cloud resources, it is possible to buy less hardware and use cloud nodes only for peak periods.

8 Conclusion

In this paper, we have presented a cloud deployment model for an HPC application. Moreover, a parallel framework for the HPC application ZaKo3D has been developed which enables the application to run on a number of cloud nodes, thus easing the migrating process of HPC application from existed on-premises resources into the cloud. The advantage of running HPC applications in the cloud environment is that using on-demand cloud resources can reduce the cost of maintenance and save on purchase of the software and equipment. But existing HPC applications are not always expected to be able to be taken entirely into a cloud environment, due to current HPC Cluster' dominant position. Therefore, we also present a combined HPC mode in which HPC applications can use cloud and on-premises resources together.

We conduct a set of experiments to compare performance between cloud and on-premises resources on the Azure platform and Cluster. In addition, applied scenarios of the two kinds of cloud modes are analyzed by results of our experiments. This work can give a reference to SMEs (small and medium-sized enterprises) to develop their HPC applications in cloud environments. We have to point out that although cloud can leverage the enterprise's HPC application development, current cloud power can only be used to supply to the status when an organization does not have enough on-premises resources to support its development, due to the capability of current cloud cannot catch up with on-premises HPC resources.

Considering our future research, for the parallel framework, we will tune application with respect to load balancing, and find a solution for the overhead in the parallel scheduler. Furthermore, based on our performance analysis of the cluster and the cloud, in the next step we will investigate the total costs (including procurement, maintenance and manpower effort) of cluster and cloud, through comparing differences between these two platforms, figure out an available rule for users to make the best decision to choose HPC platforms in rational combination of the price and performance within their capability. In addition, we will implement the combined HPC mode.

References

1. Amazon's Elastic Compute Cloud. http://aws.amazon.com/ec2/
2. IBM SmartCloud. http://www.ibm.com/cloud-computing/us/en/
3. Google Apps. http://www.google.com/apps/intl/en/business/cloud.html
4. Microsoftware Windows Azure. http://www.windowsazure.com/en-us/
5. Costaa, P., Cruzb, A.: Migration to Windows Azure-analysis and comparison. In: CENTERIS 2012 - Conference on ENTERprise Information Systems/HCIST 2012 – International Conference on Health and Social Care Information Systems and Technologies. Procedia Technol. **5**, 93–102 (2012)
6. Mondéjar, R., Pedro, C., Carles, P., Lluis, P.: CloudSNAP: a transparent infrastructure for decentralized web deployment using distributed interception. Future Gener. Comput. Syst. **29**, 370–380 (2013)
7. Marozzo, F., Lordan, F., Rafanell, R., Lezzi, D., Talia, D., Badia, R.M.: Enabling cloud interoperability with COMPSs. In: Kaklamanis, C., Papatheodorou, T., Spirakis, P.G. (eds.) Euro-Par 2012. LNCS, vol. 7484, pp. 16–27. Springer, Heidelberg (2012)
8. HPC scheduler. Windows Azure HPC scheduler. http://msdn.microsoft.com/en-us/library/hh560247(v=vs.85).aspx. Windows Azure. http://www.microsoft.com/windowsazure/
9. Brecher, C., Gorgels, C., Kauffmann, P., Röthlingshöfer, T., Flodin, A., Henser, J.: ZaKo3D-simulation possibilities for PM gears. In: World Congress on Powder Metal, Florenz (2010)
10. http://www.wzl.rwth-aachen.de/en/index.htm
11. Hpccloud. Google Enters IaaS Cloud Race. http://www.hpcinthecloud.com/hpccloud/2012-07-03/google_enters_iaas_cloud_race.html
12. Penguin Computing on Demand. http://www.penguincomputing.com/services/hpc-cloud/POD
13. Sabalcore HPC Cloud Service. http://www.sabalcore.com/why_on_demand.html
14. UniCloud. http://www.univa.com/products/unicloud.php
15. R-Cloud. http://www.r-hpc.com/
16. SGI cyclone. http://www.sgi.com/products/?/cyclone/

Author Index